AUNTY ACID'S
GUIDE TO LOVE
CREATED BY GED BACKLAND

GIBBS SMITH
TO ENRICH AND INSPIRE HUMANKIND

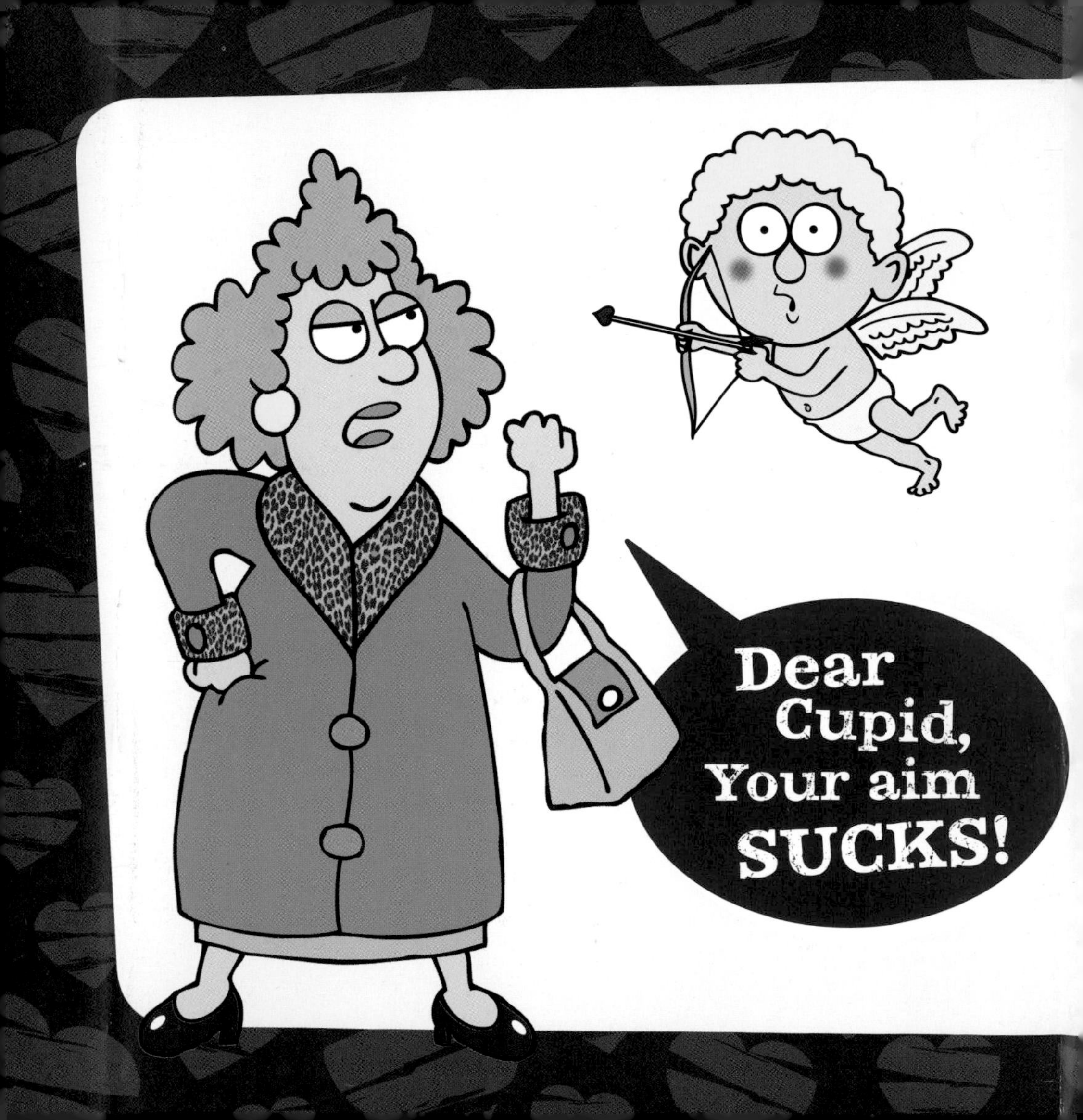
Dear Cupid, Your aim SUCKS!

HELLO, FRIENDS...

Welcome to my little book on all matters of the heart, as some famous band once said,

"ALL YOU NEED IS LOVE."

I followed this mantra, and I tried paying my mortgage with a hug once, but for some reason it didn't fly with the bank.

I've had my share of love and romance—some good, some bad—but mostly funny (have you seen my husband Walt?).

So have a peep inside for pages and pages of my witty words on love, sex and marriage. Plus musings on why men are like buses—not to be chased after as there will be another along at any minute.

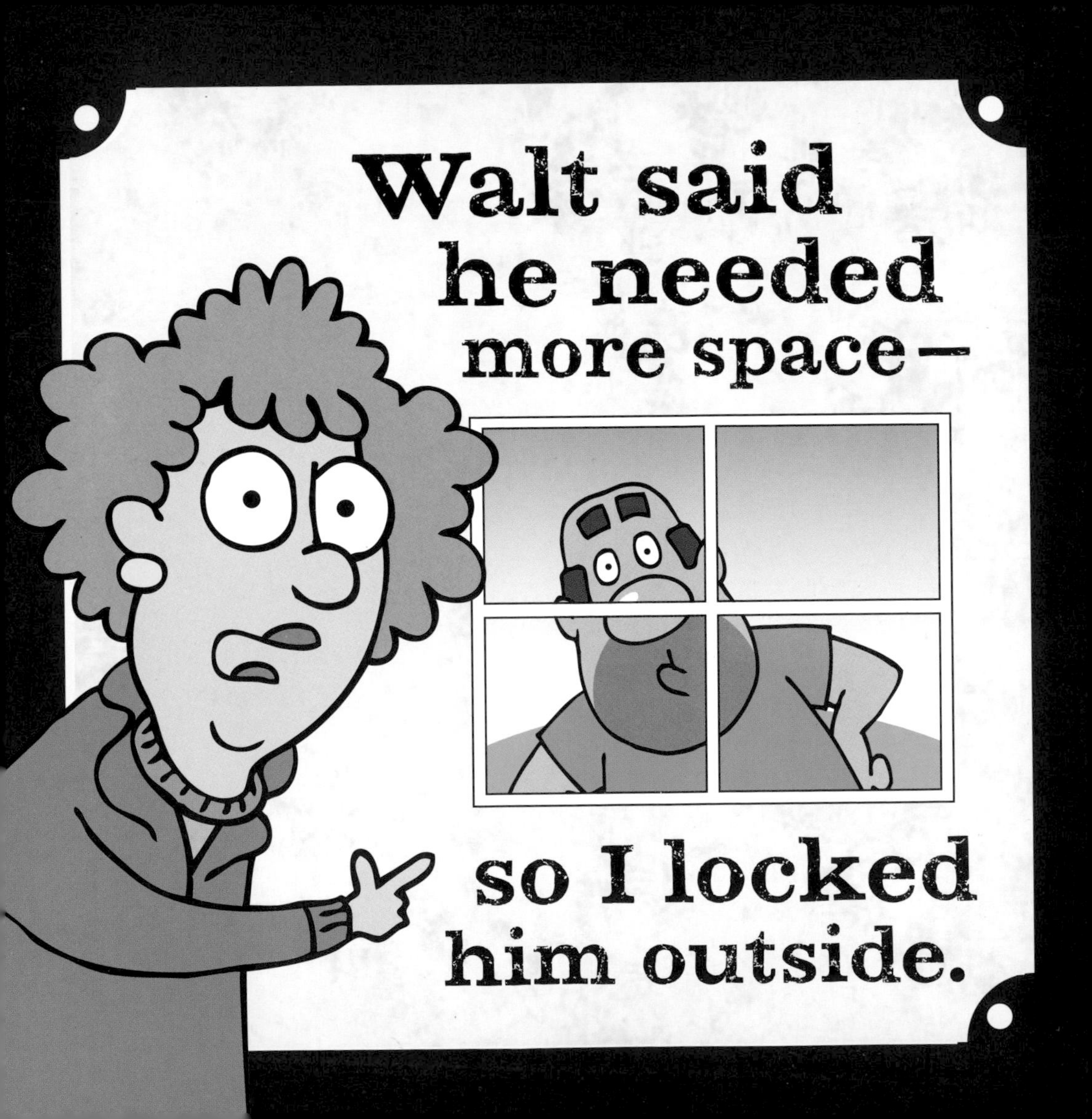
Walt said
he needed
more space—
so I locked
him outside.

If absence makes the heart grow fonder, some people I know haven't been gone freakin' long enough.

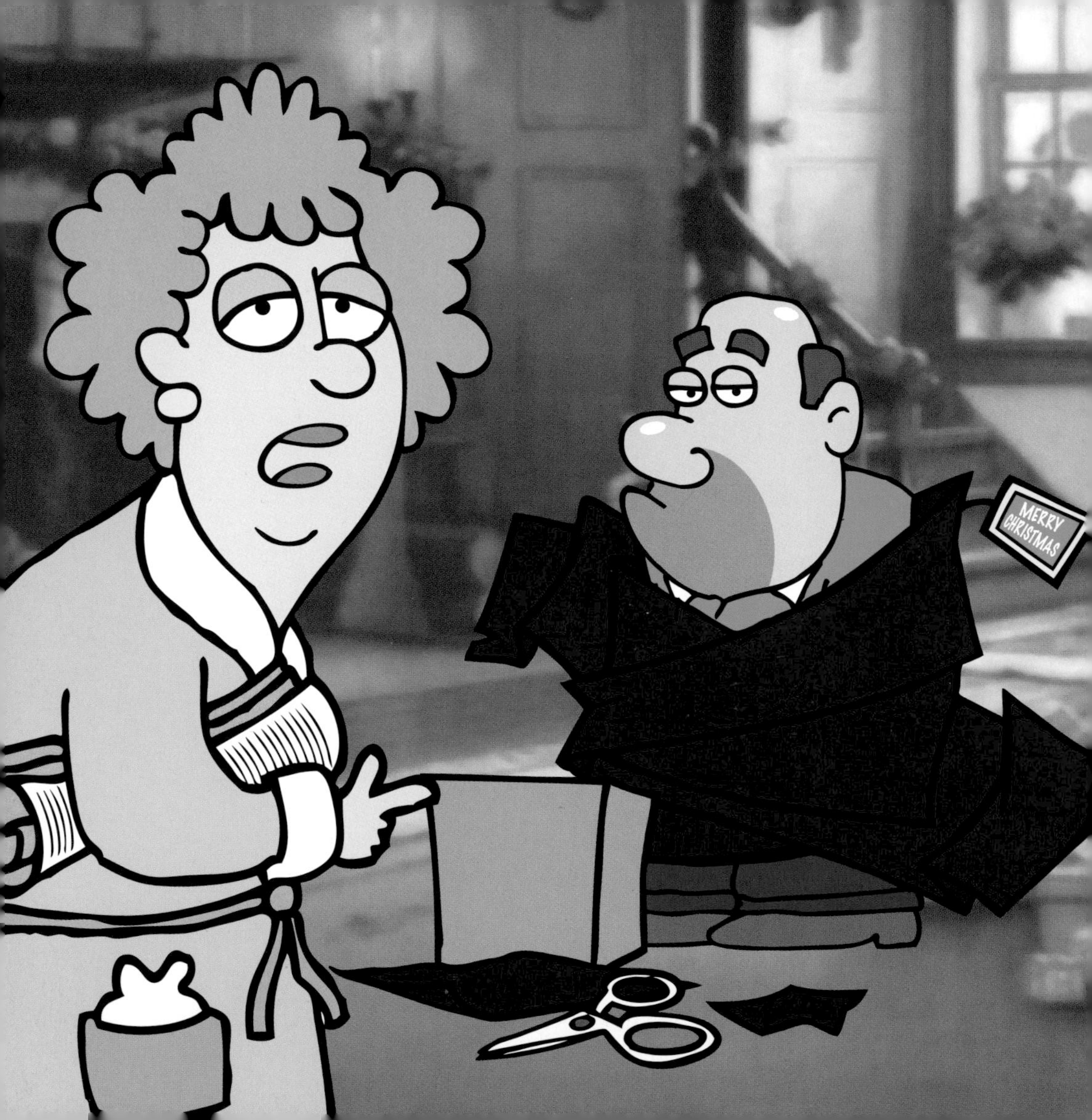
MERRY CHRISTMAS

Anyone who thinks
men and women
are equal
has never seen
a man trying
to wrap a
Christmas
present.

I have finally found *Love*...

The aisle signed "candy" at the store.

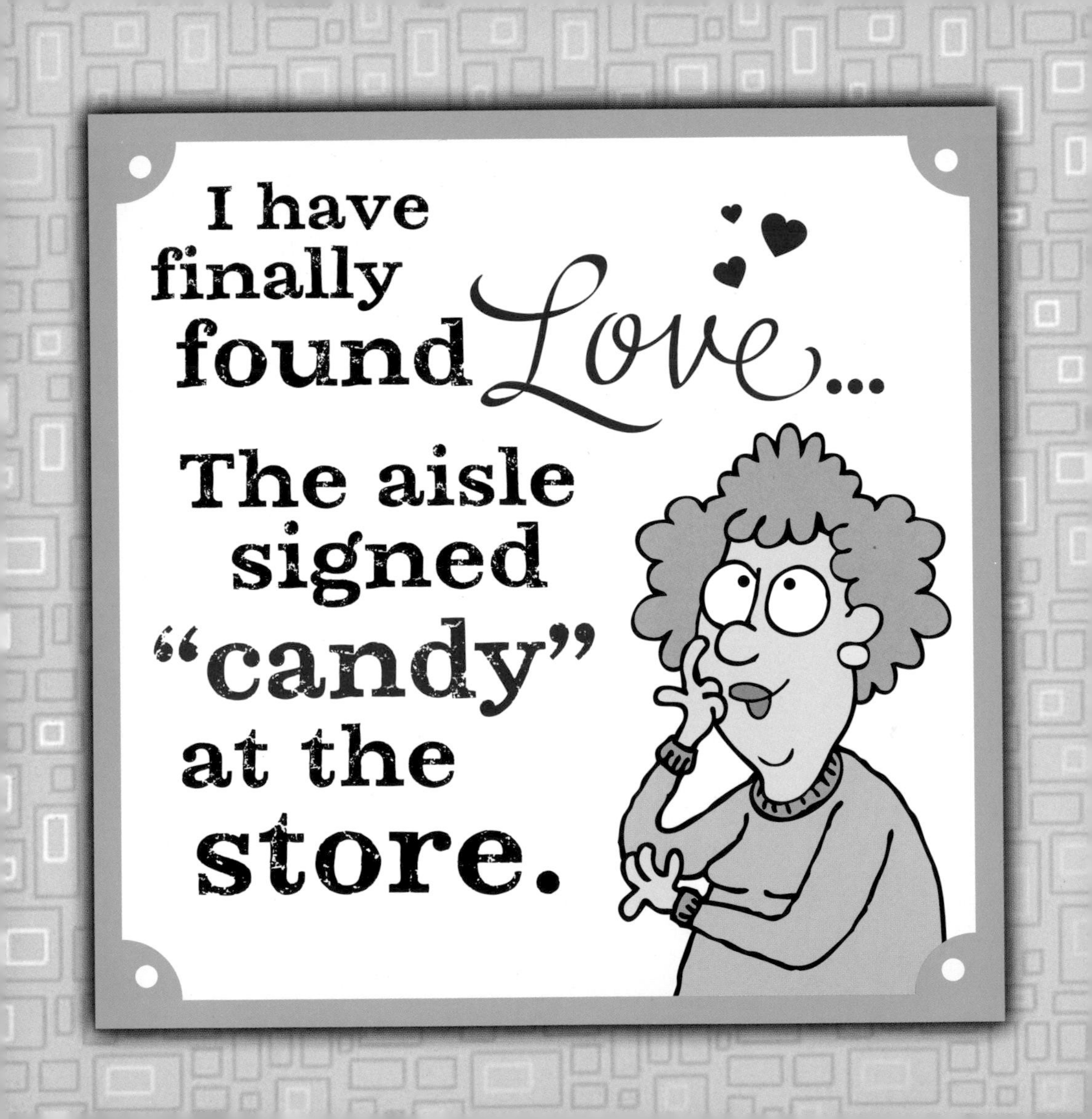

Men say that **women** should come with **instructions.**

What's the point?

Have you ever seen a man actually read them?

AUNTY ACID'S
ADVICE FOR MEN
NO.28

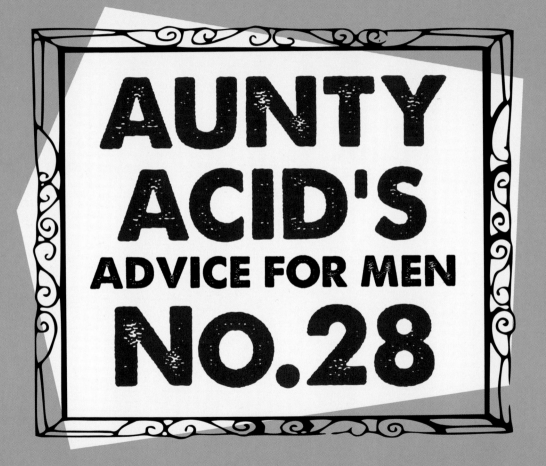

When a woman says, "Do whatever you want." DO NOT, under any circumstances, do whatever you want.

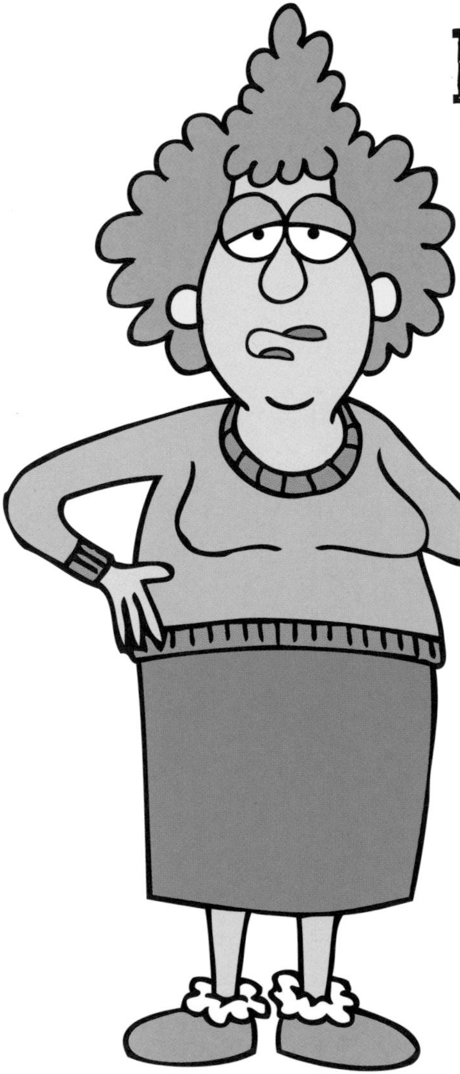

I tell Walt
I'm still
hot...
but
nowadays
it's just in
flashes.

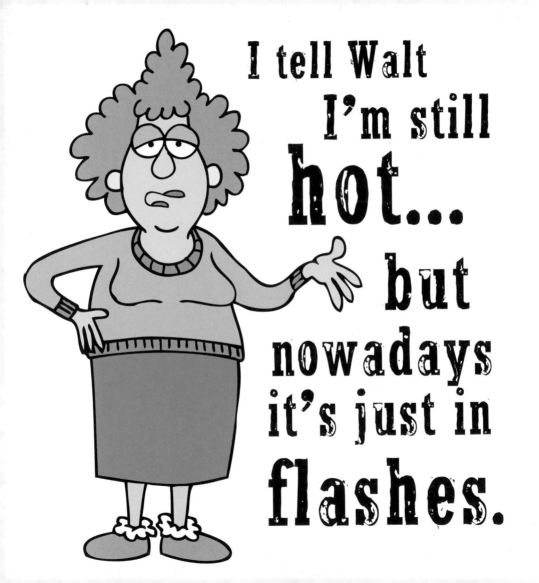

Some Men
are a habit
you should
kick...
...with both
feet...
...down a flight
of freakin'
stairs.

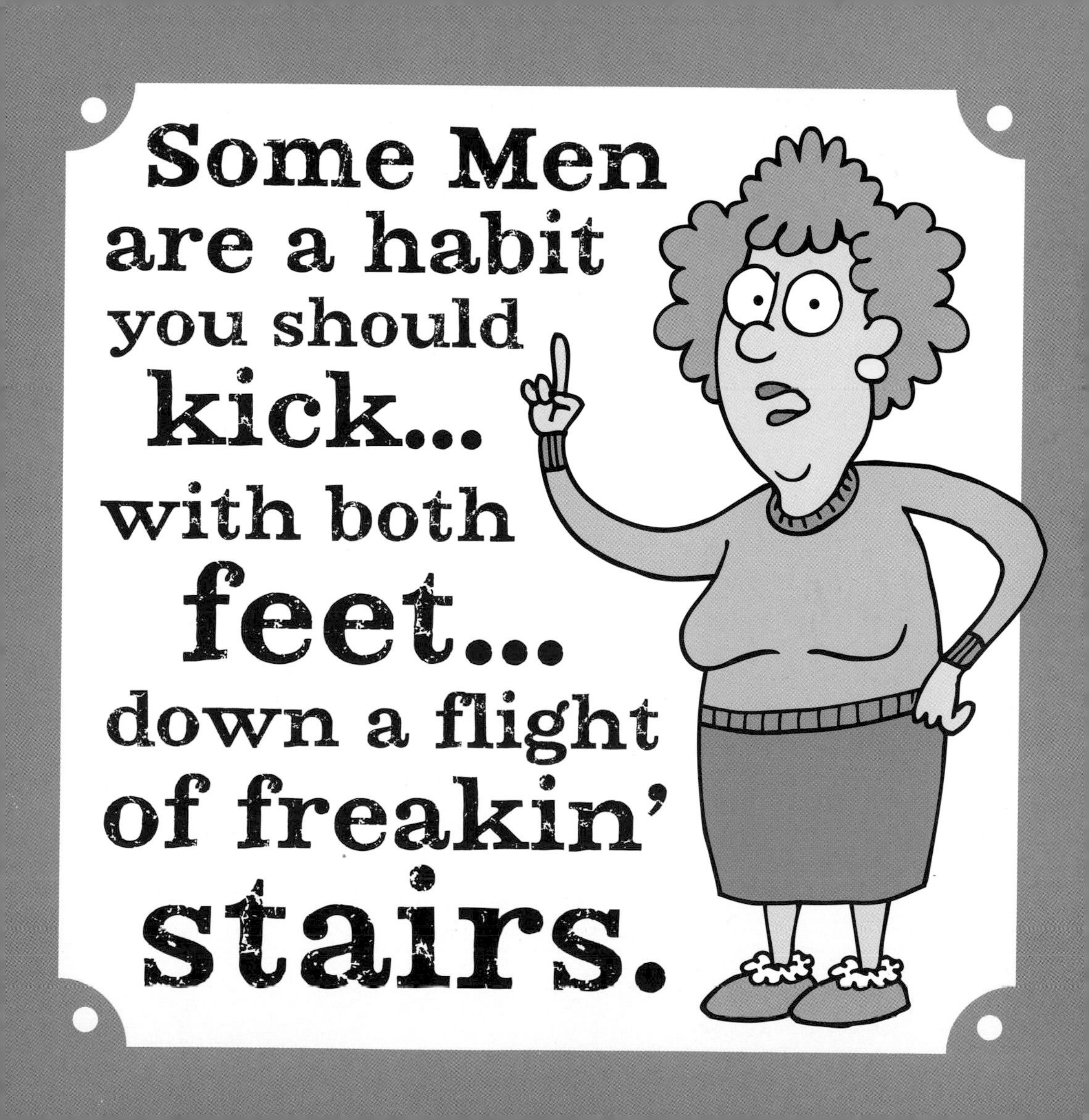

I enjoy long, romantic walks...

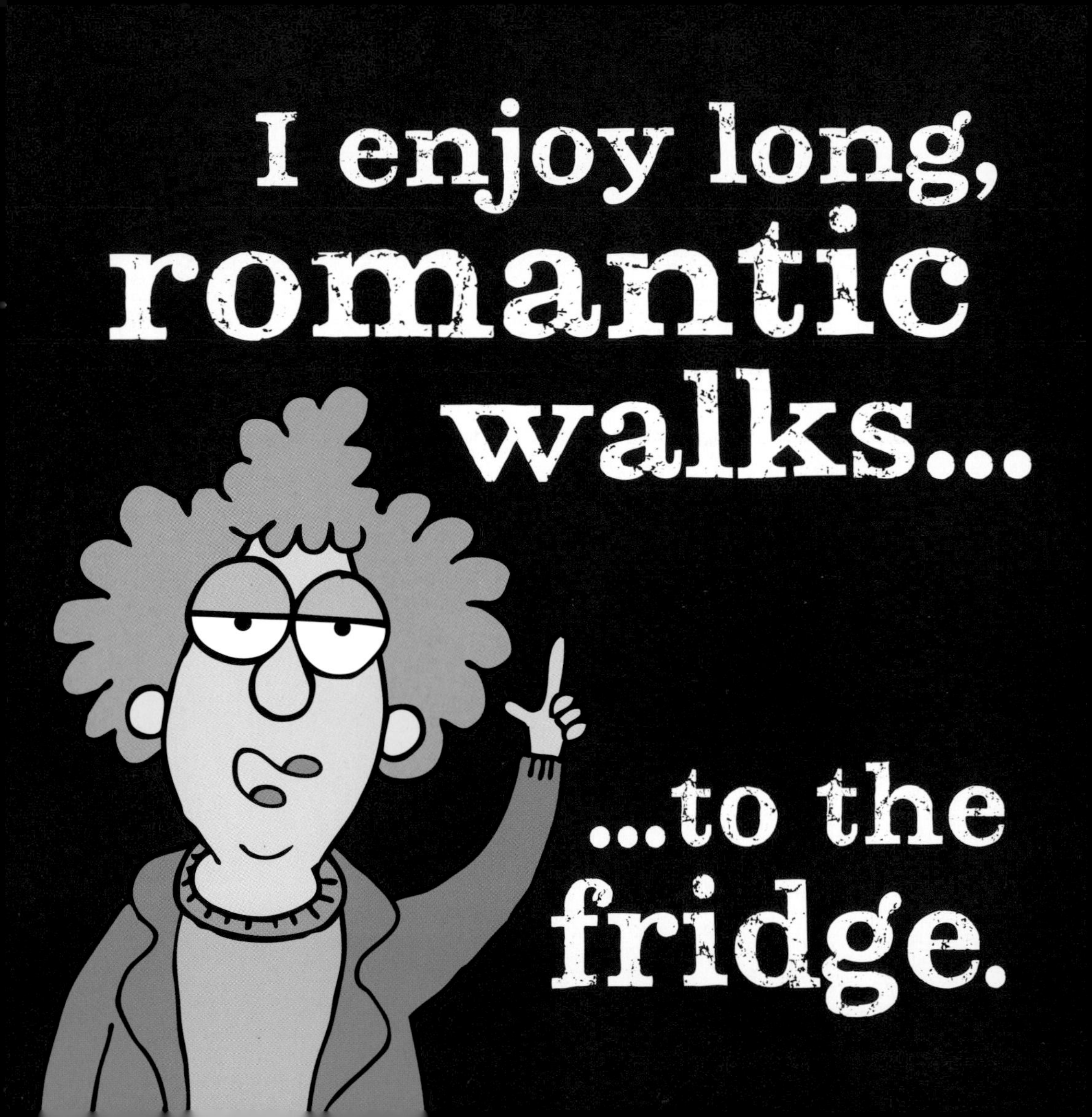

...to the fridge.

Remember ladies,
if a guy
whistles
at you,
don't turn
your head,
you're a
lady
not a
dog.

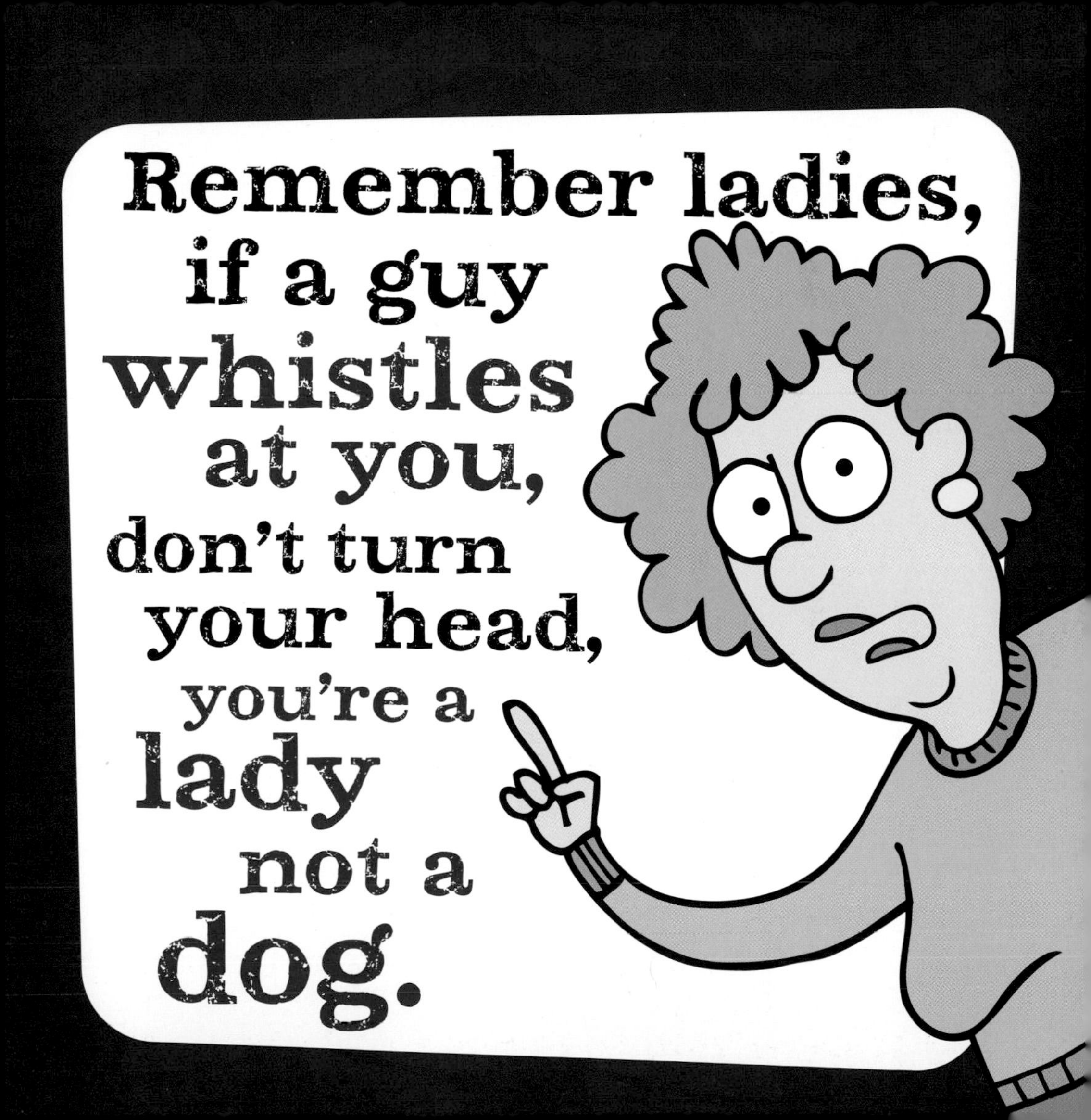

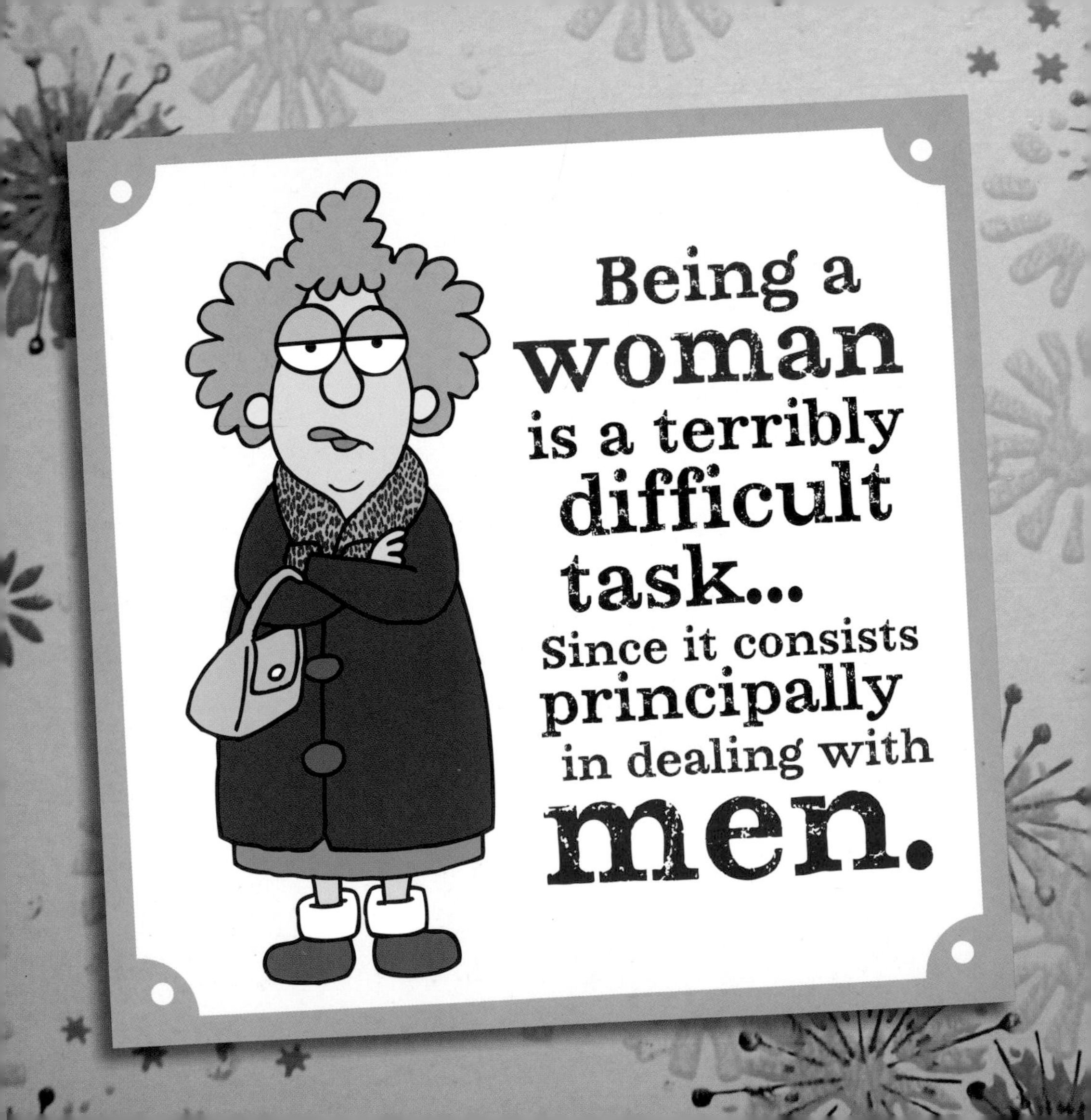
Being a
woman
is a terribly
difficult
task...
Since it consists
principally
in dealing with
men.

I hate it when you
offer someone a sincere
compliment
about their
mustache
and
suddenly
...she's not
your friend
anymore.

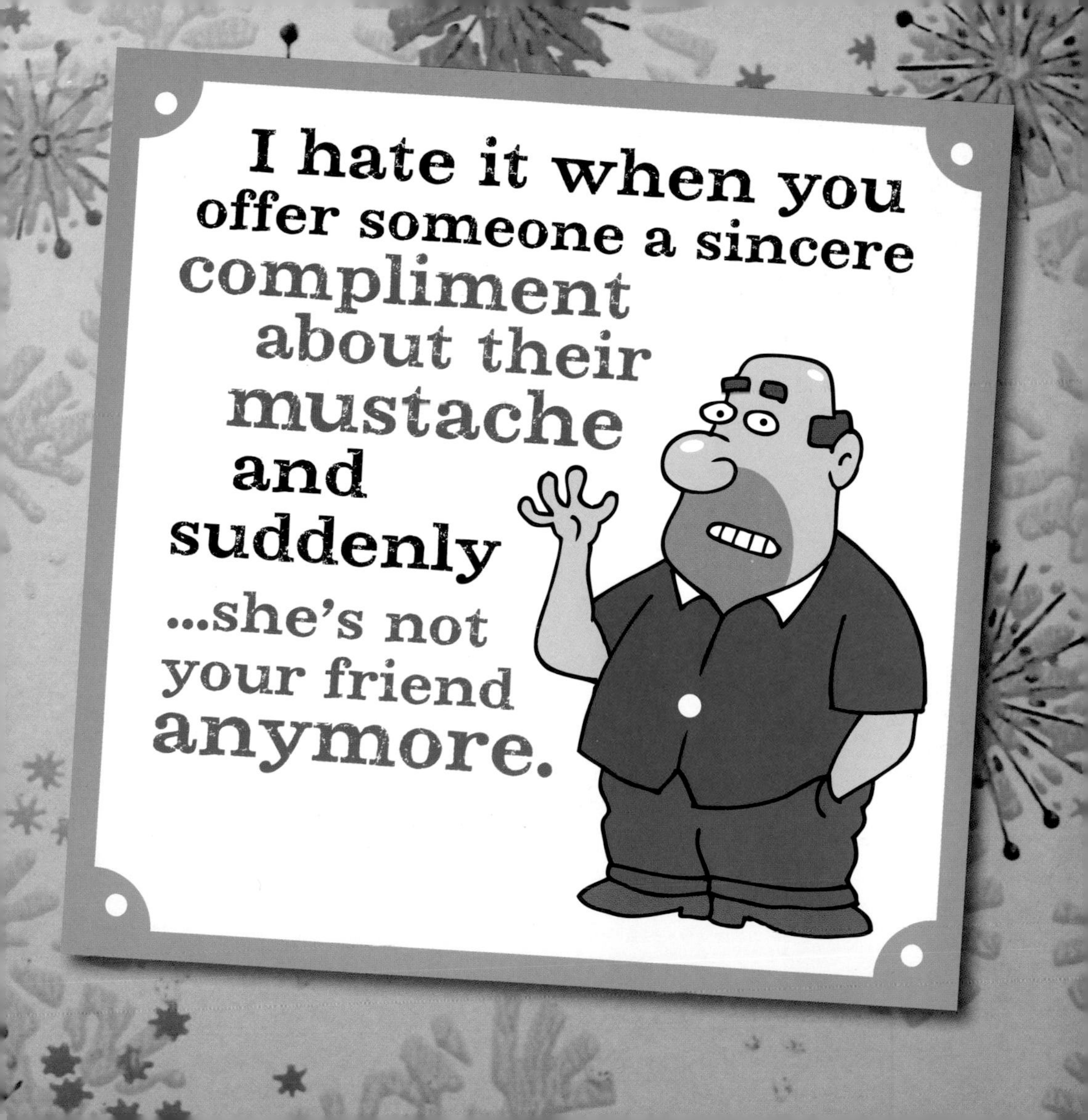

The only thing a woman should ever chase is her vodka.

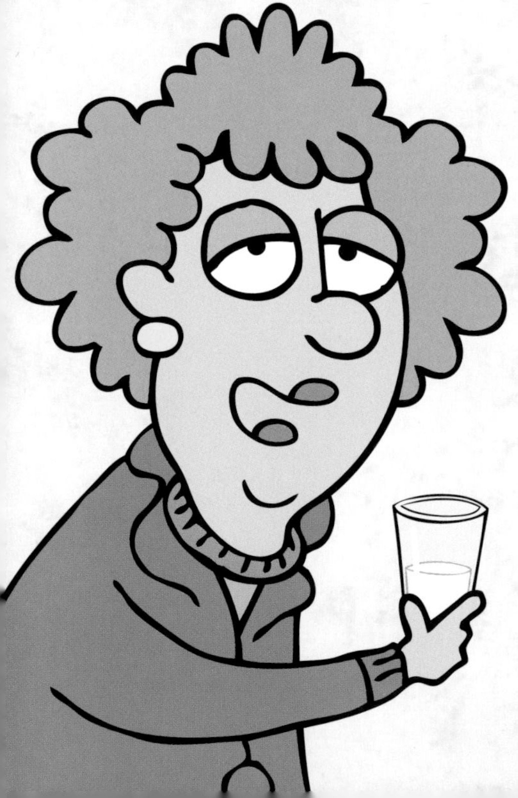

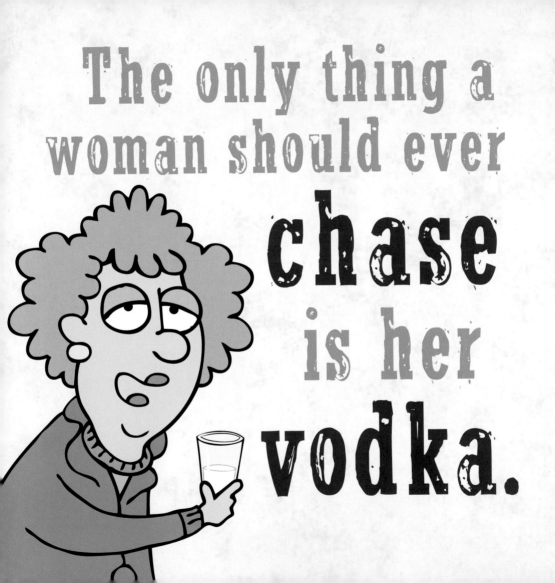

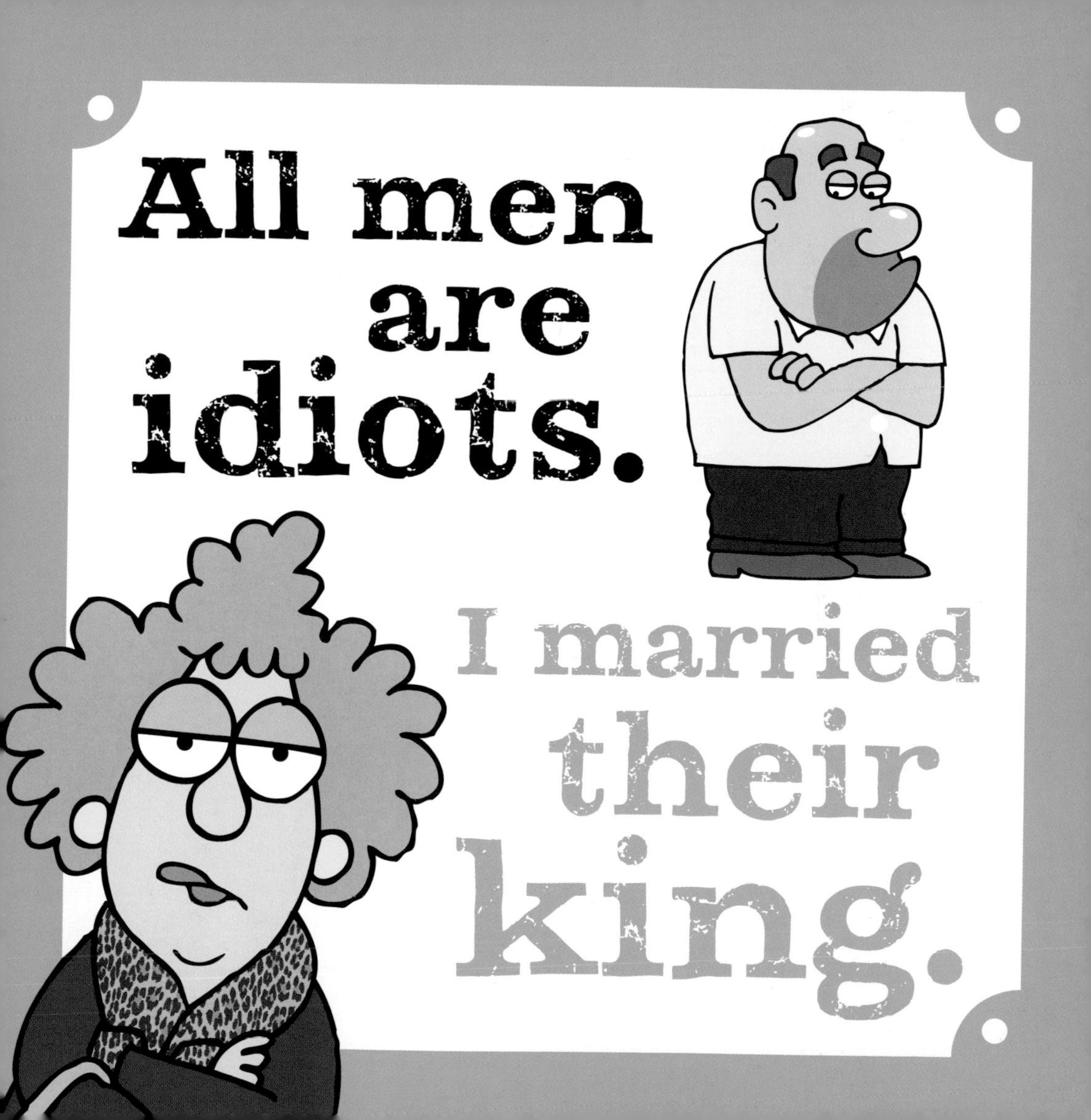
All men are idiots.
I married their king.

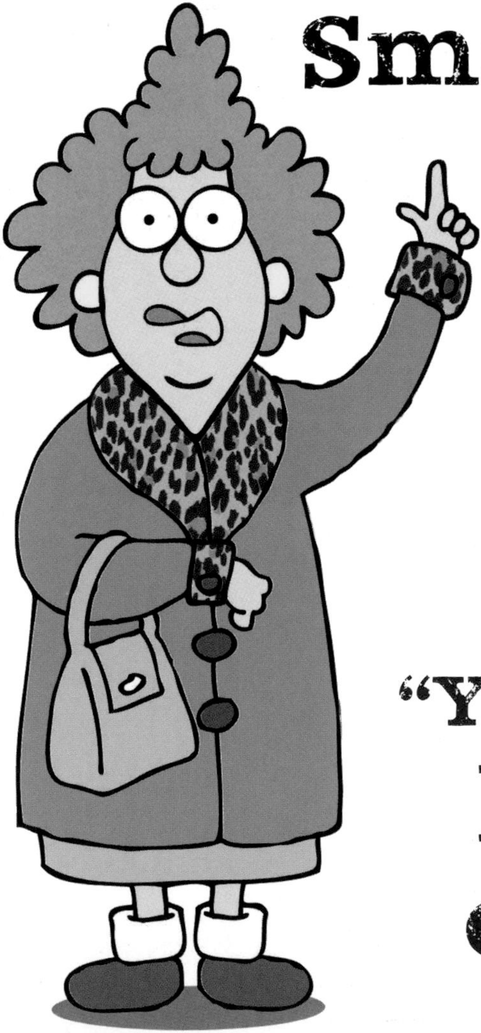

Smart ladies
don't have
"exes"
they have
"Ys"
as in—
"Y the freakin'
hell did I
do that?"

So then they handcuffed me and said, "Anthing you say can and will be held against you."

So I said, "Johnny Depp."

Aunty told me to go out and get something that makes her look sexy.

So I'm off out to get drunk.

Of course **women** don't work as hard as men.

They get it right first time.

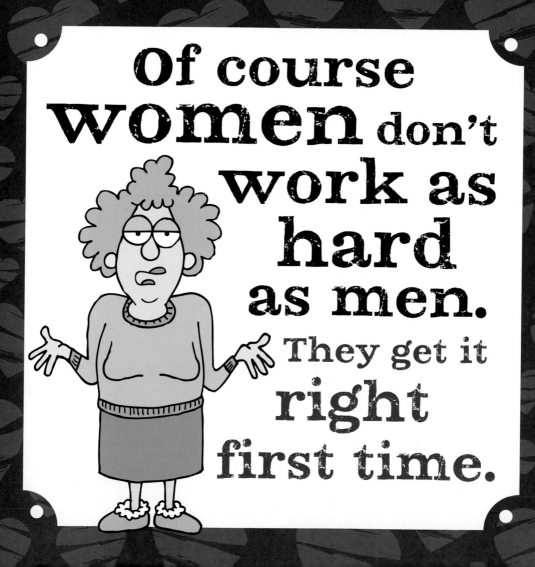

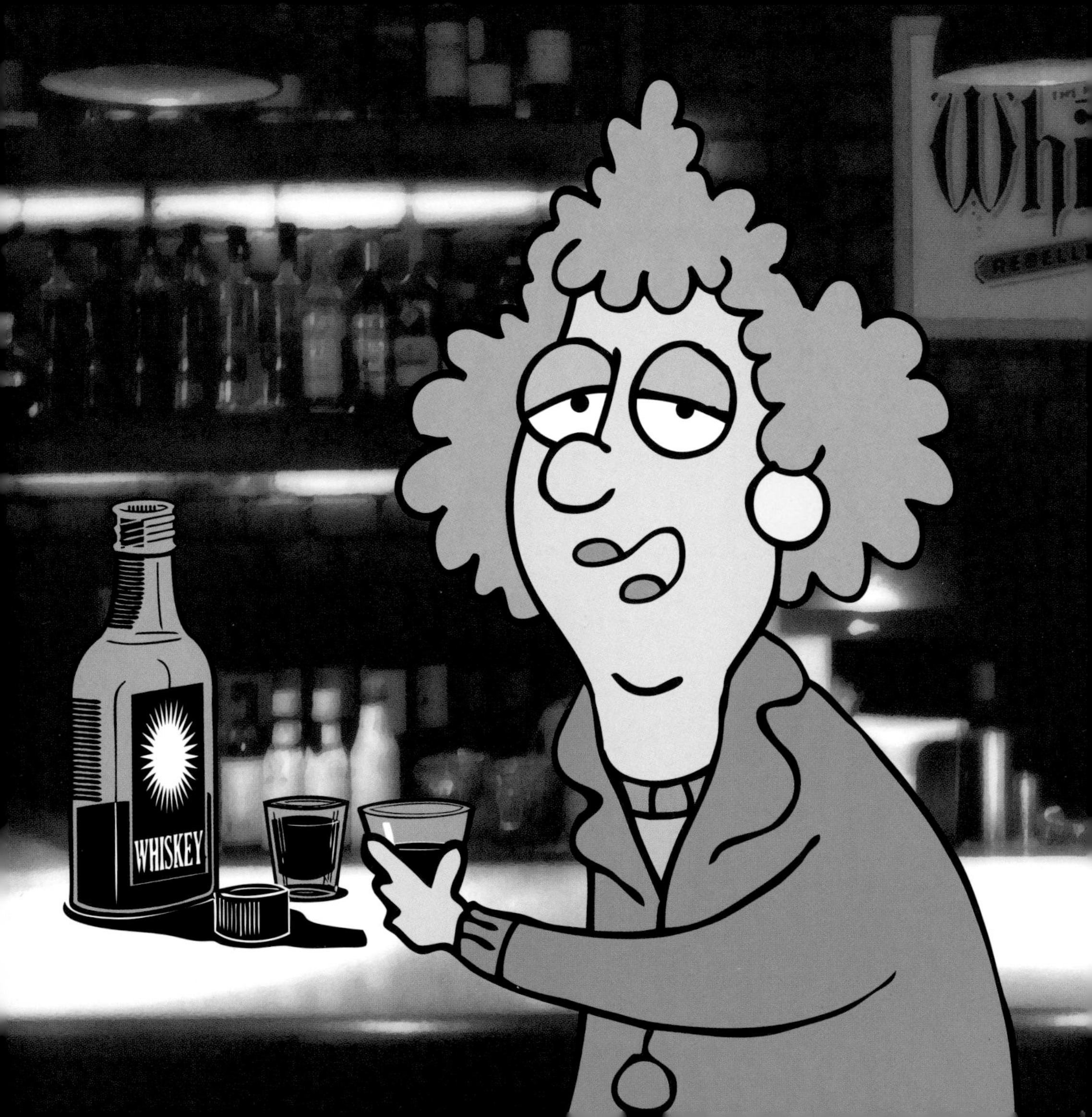
WHISKEY

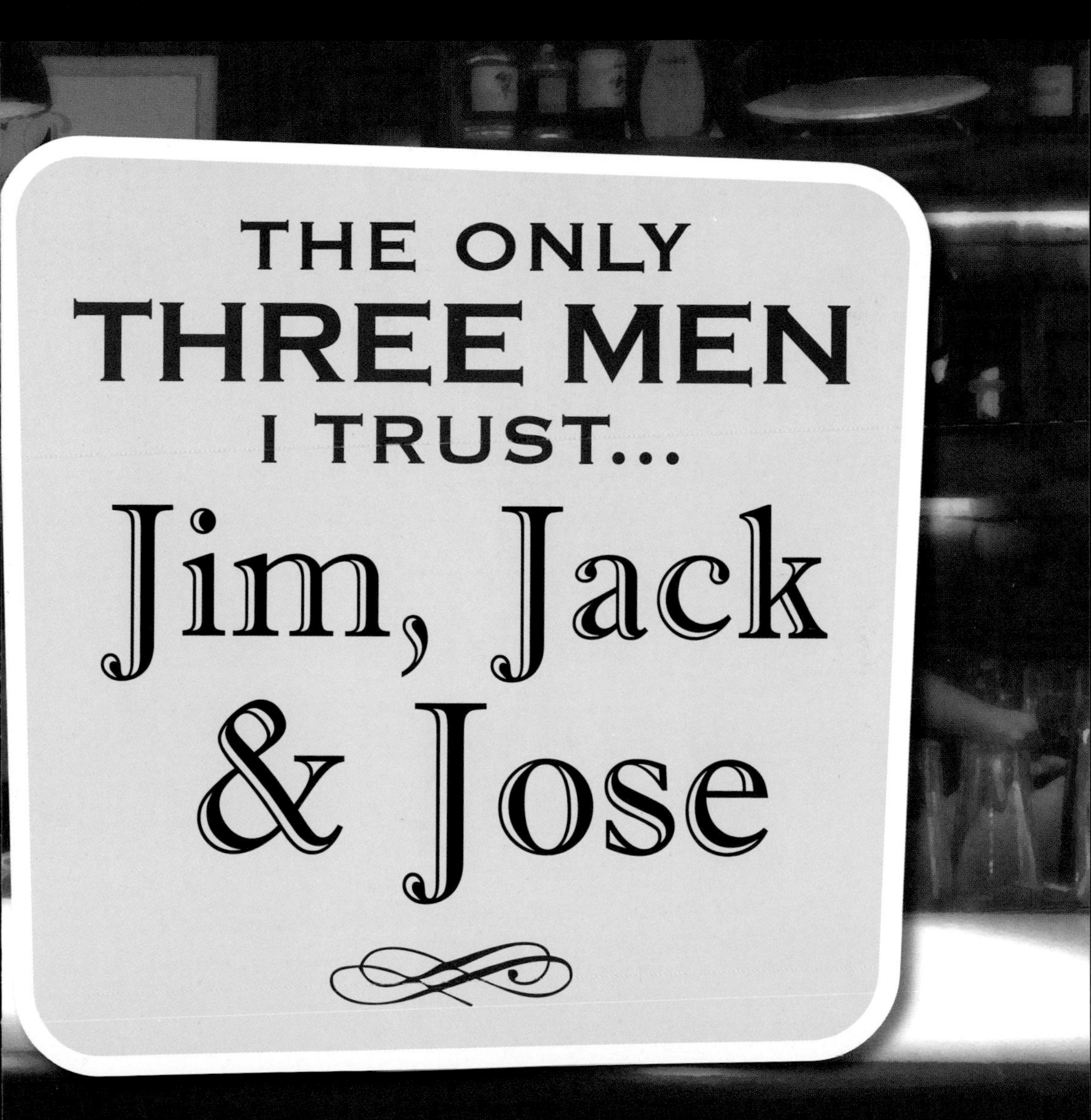
THE ONLY
THREE MEN
I TRUST...
Jim, Jack
& Jose

Relationships

are like **fat people.** Most of them don't **work out.**

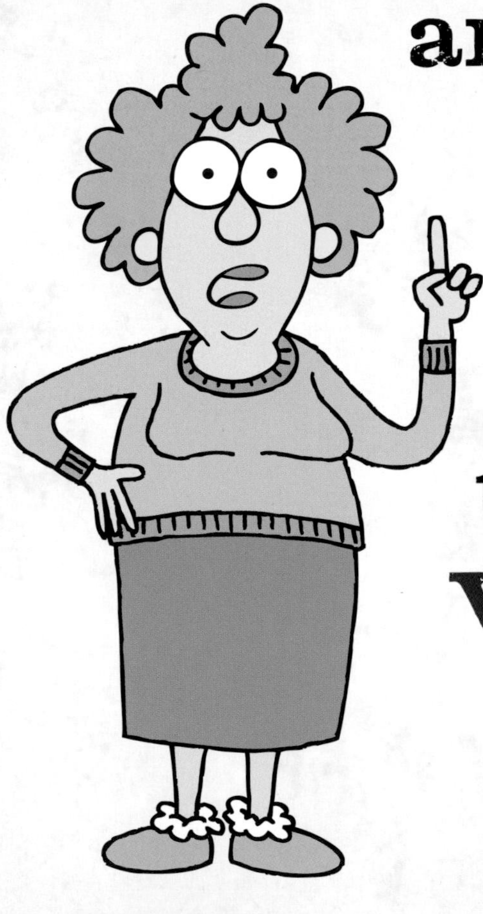

Marriage: The only war where you sleep with the enemy.

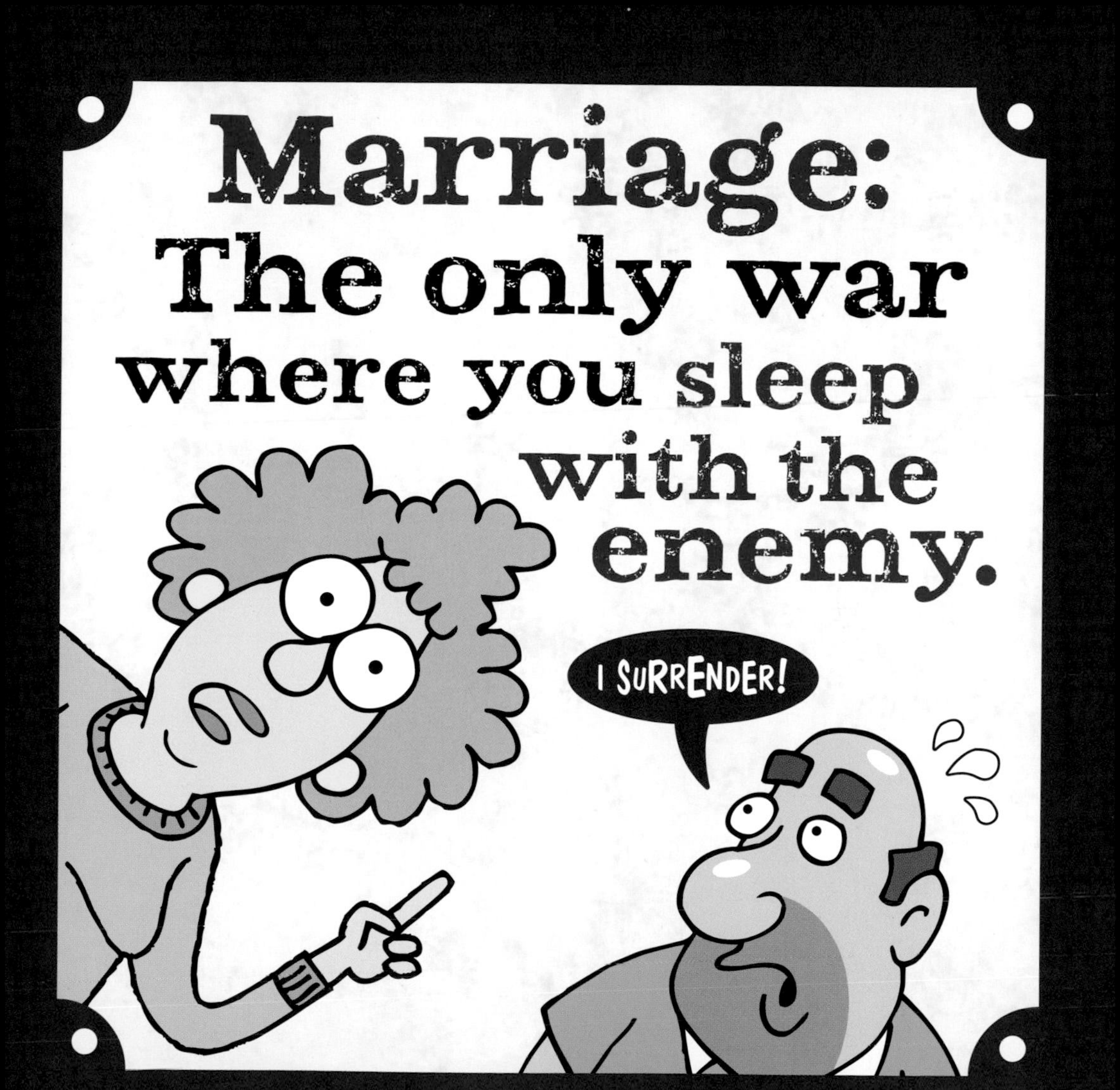
I SURRENDER!

My relationship
is perfect
as my man
does this
cute thing...
...where
he doesn't
exist.

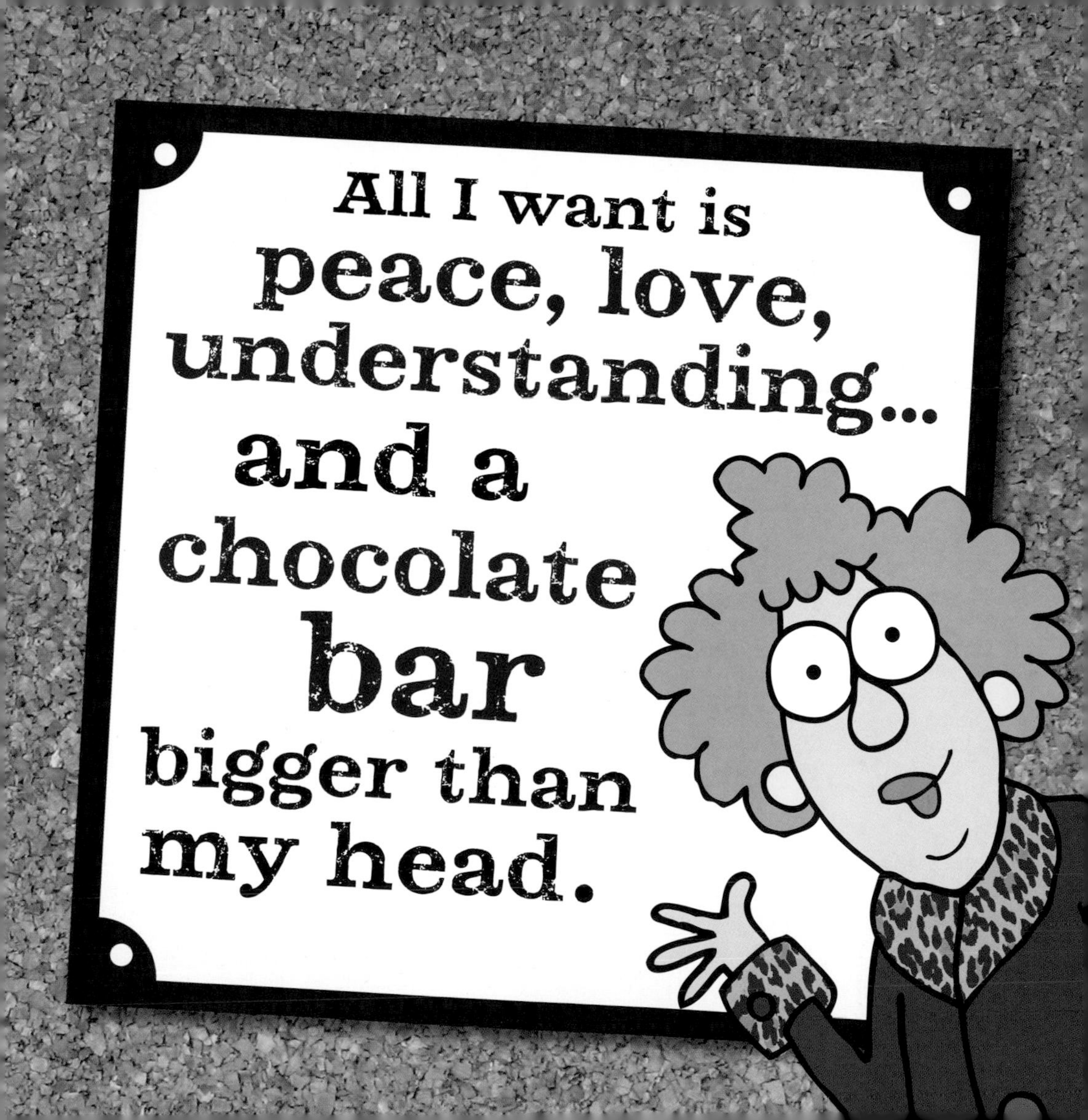
All I want is
peace, love,
understanding...
and a
chocolate
bar
bigger than
my head.

AUNTY ACID'S GUIDE TO LOVE AND A LASTING RELATIONSHIP

1. Find a man who makes you laugh.
2. Find a man who has a good job and can cook.
3. Find a man who is honest.
4. Find a man who will pamper you with gifts.
5. Find a man who is awesome in bed.
6. MOST IMPORTANT OF ALL–
It is very important that these 5 men
NEVER MEET!

Getting married for **SEX** is like buying a jumbo jet for the **free** peanuts.

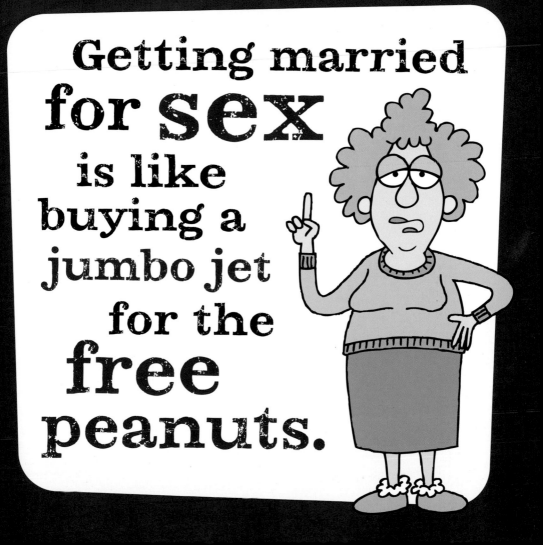

There is someone out there for everyone, however, for some people that person might be five cats.

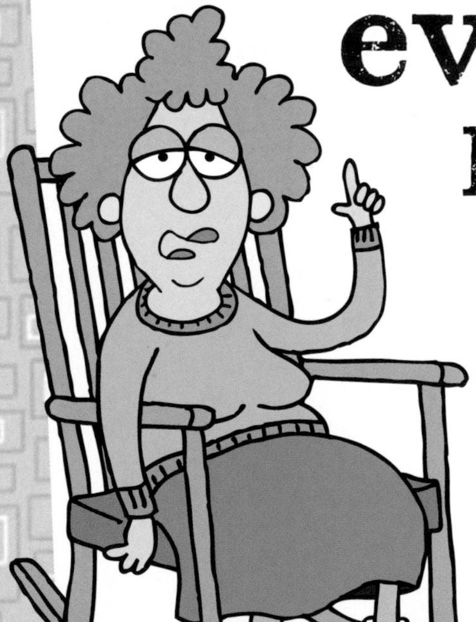

MARRIAGE IS A RELATIONSHIP IN WHICH ONE PERSON IS ALWAYS RIGHT... AND THE OTHER IS USUALLY THE HUSBAND.

I love watching people fall in love. There's nothing like having that special someone who thinks you're beautiful no matter what.

Walt used to say he thought it was cute when I got mad, that soon ended when I got freakin' gorgeous!

Read on and you'll find many more of my whimsical words of love.

AUNTY ACID'S ADVICE FOR MEN NO.23

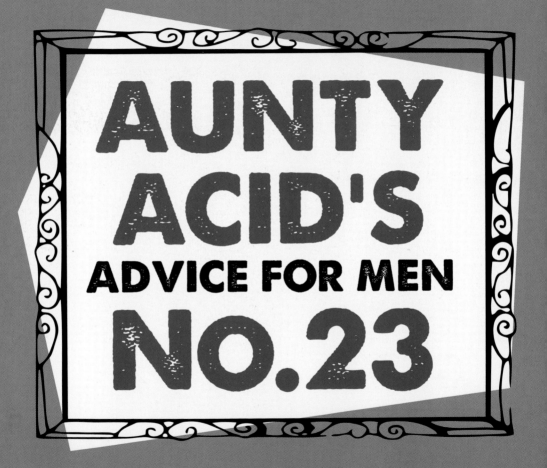

When a woman says, "What?" It's not because she didn't hear you. She's just giving you the chance to change what you said.

Why experiment on animals when there're ex-husbands?

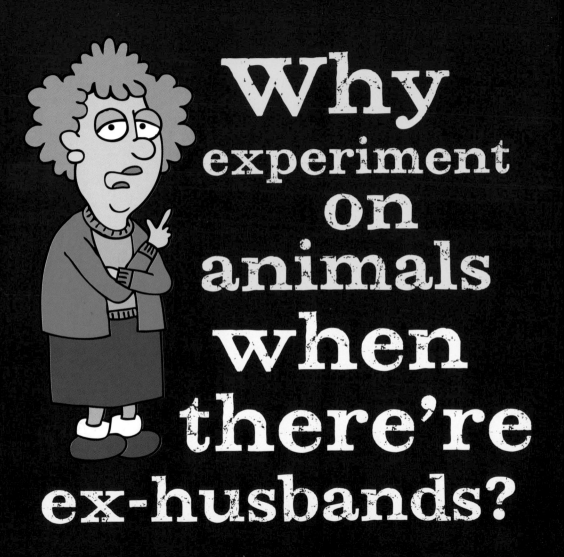

If your significant other claims they never look at your Facebook profile, change your status to single and wait five minutes.

Remember, Sisters...

CHOCOLATE is not afraid of COMMITMENT.

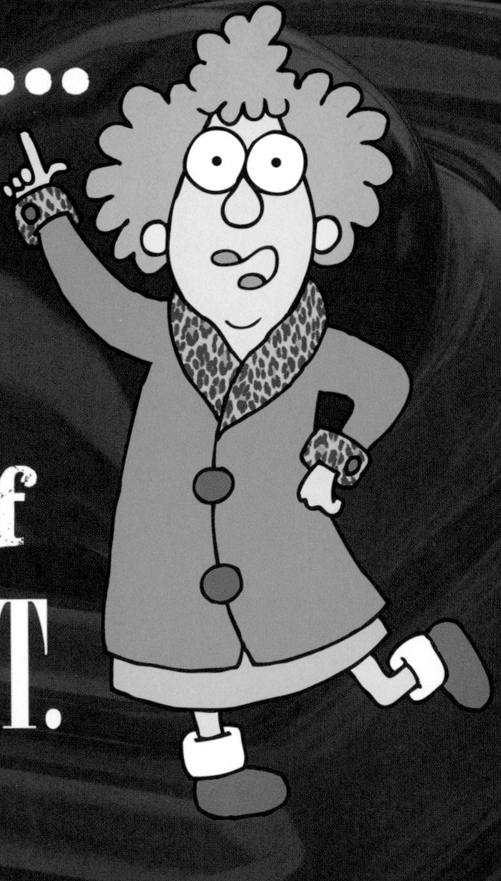

Some PEOPLE just need a HUG... around the NECK ...with a ROPE.

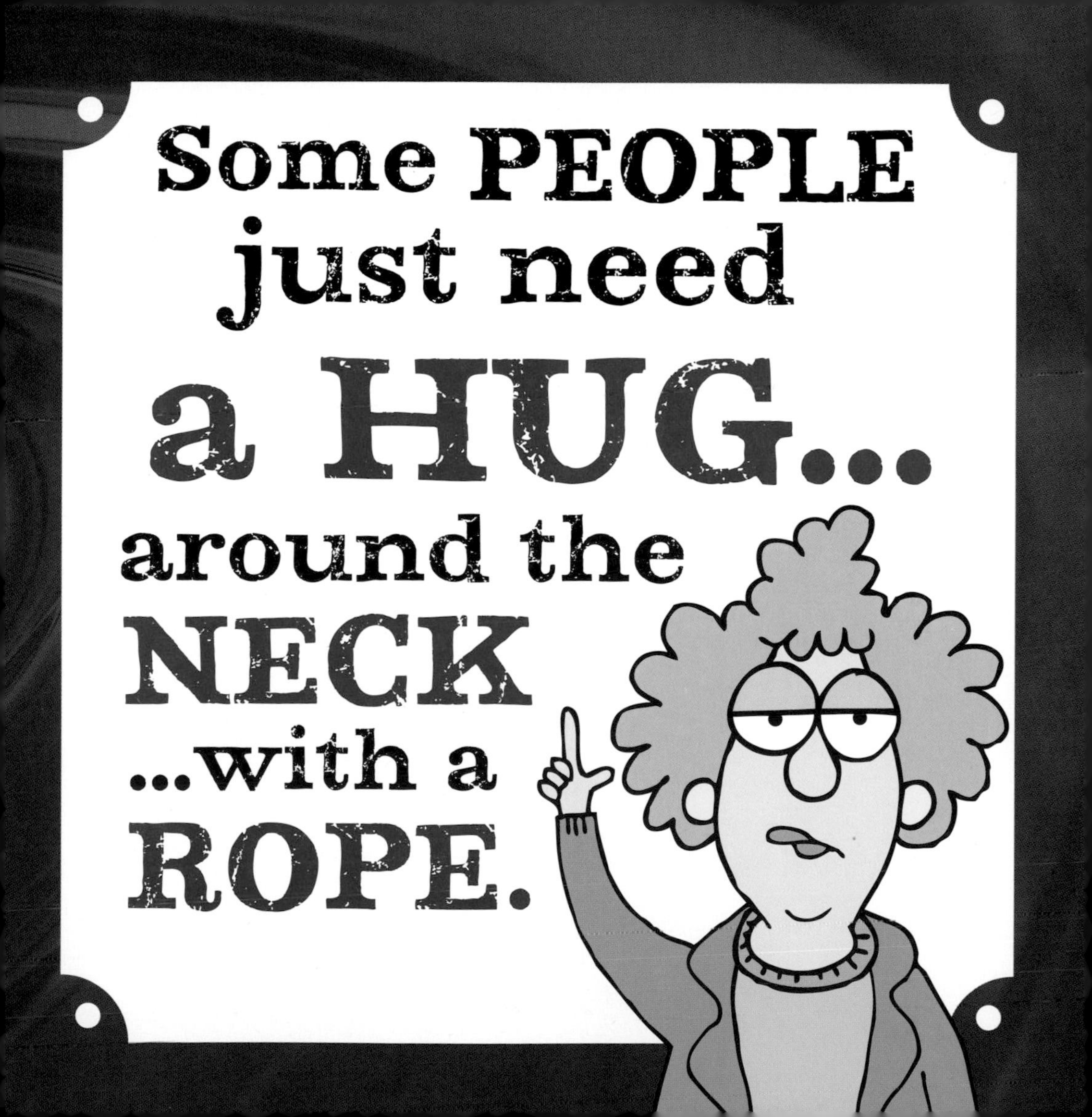

I didn't say it was your fault, I said I was blaming you.

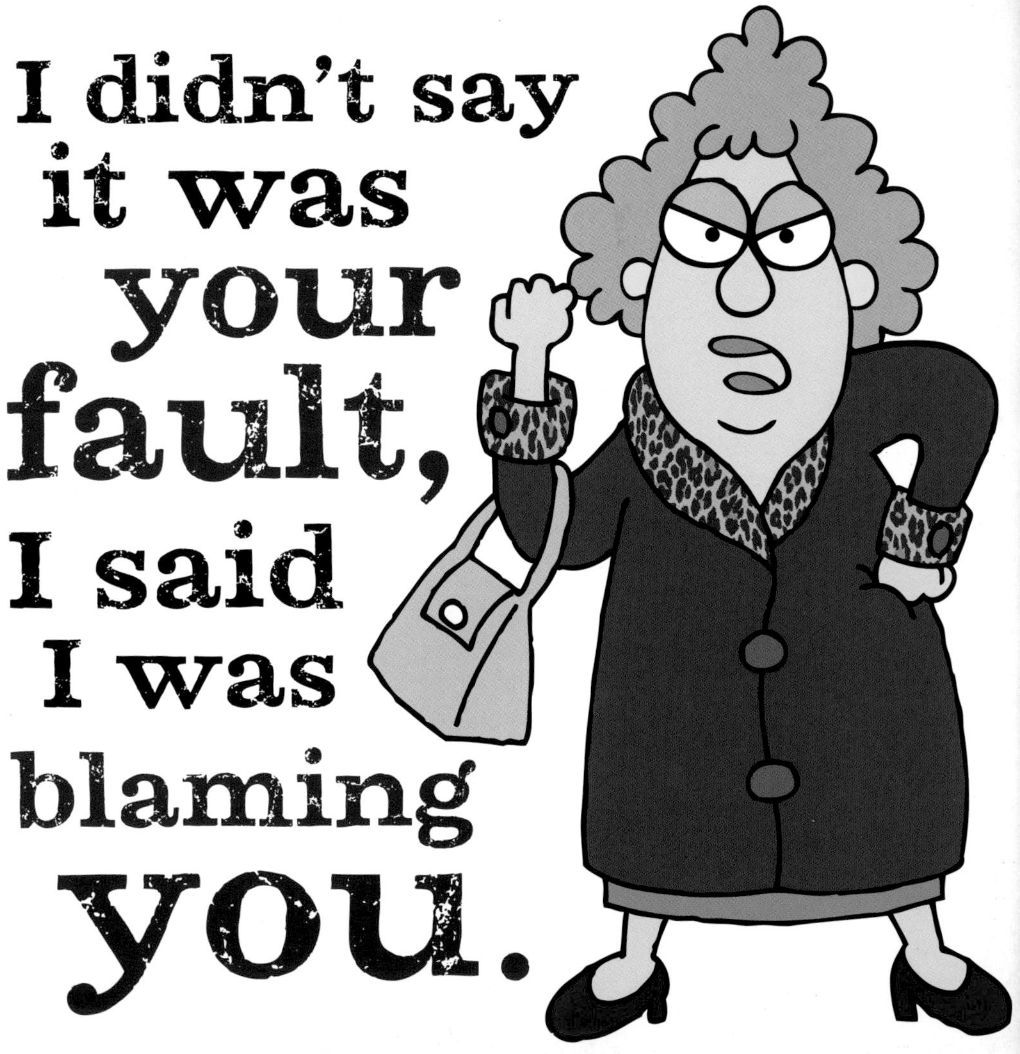

I had
a date with a
dolphin once,
it went
really
well –
WE JUST
CLICKED.

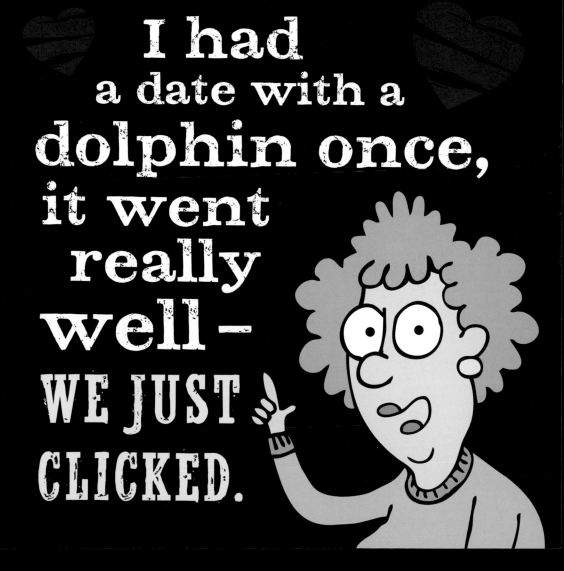

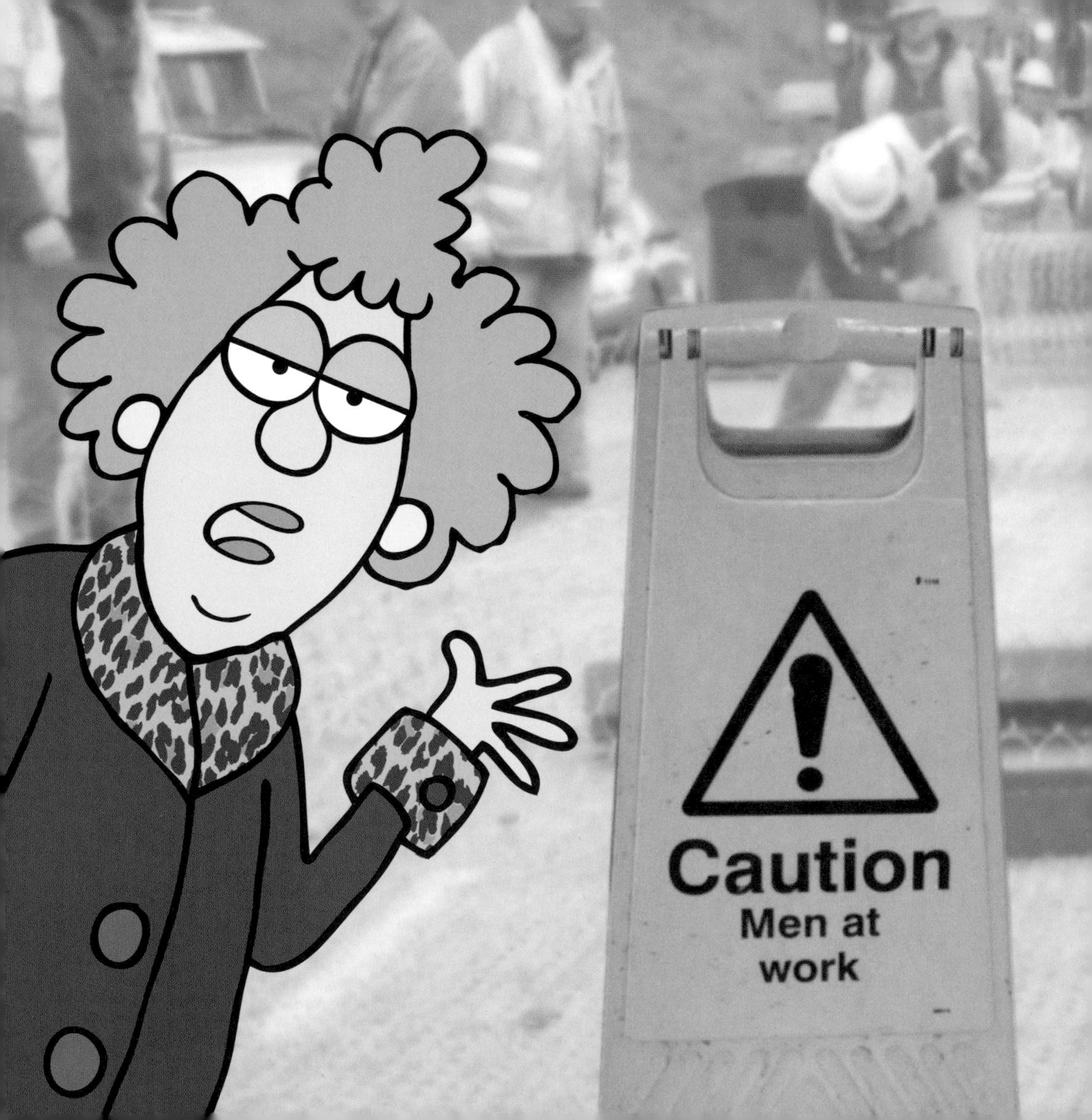
Caution
Men at
work

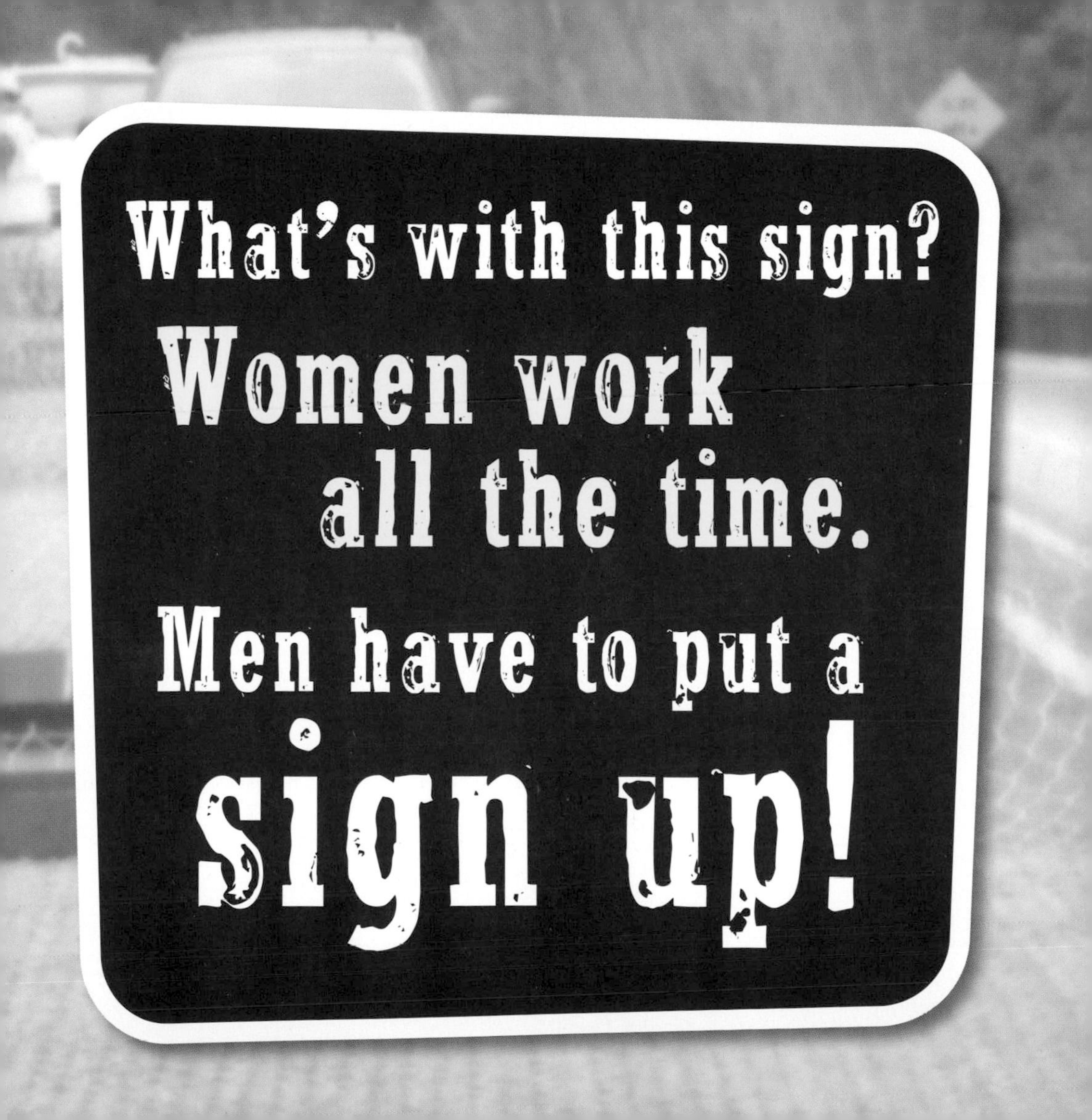
What's with this sign?
Women work
all the time.
Men have to put a
sign up!

COFFEE

A magical substance that turns, "Leave me alone or die" into, "Good morning, Honey."

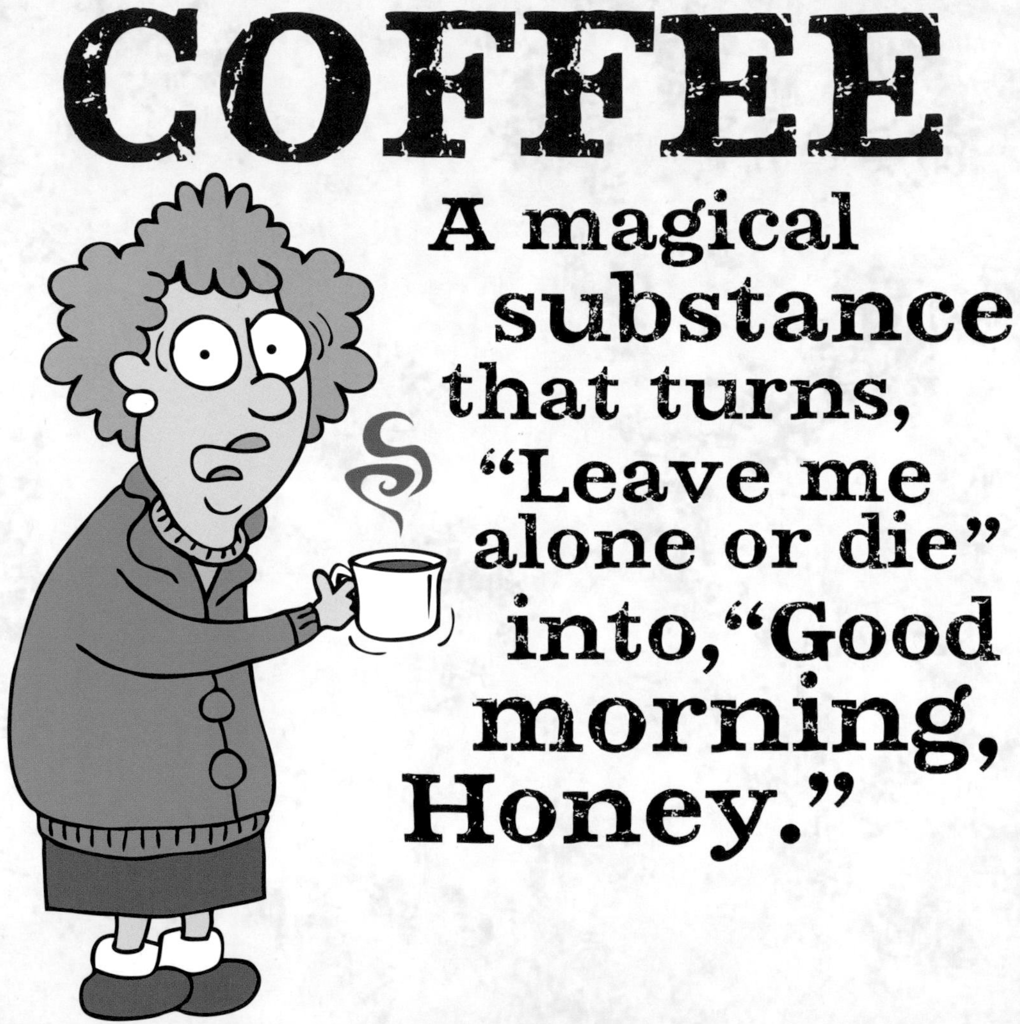

The Perfect Guy

doesn't DRINK,
doesn't SMOKE,
doesn't CHEAT...
and doesn't
EXIST.

Today I saw something which reminded me of my Ex-husband. Then I flushed it away and everything went back to normal.

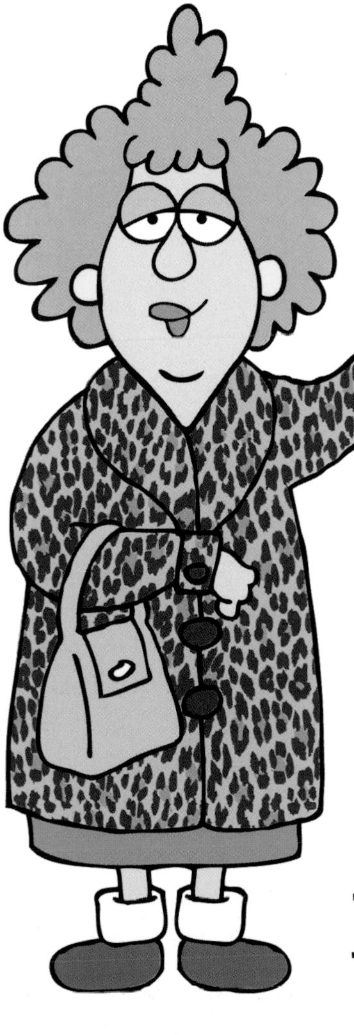

I think
Snow White
had the
right idea...
She moved
in with 7 guys
who went to
work every day
and all she had
to do was
whistle to get
the birds to do
her cleaning!

Marriage should be like a WORKSHOP where the husband WORKS and the wife SHOPS.

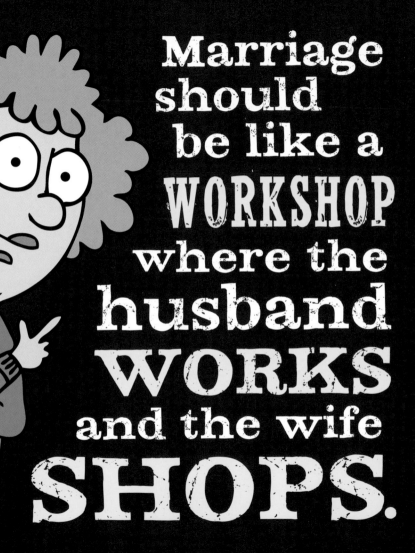

Women
are not
MOODY.
We simply
have days
when we're
less inclined
to **PUT UP**
with your
CRAP!

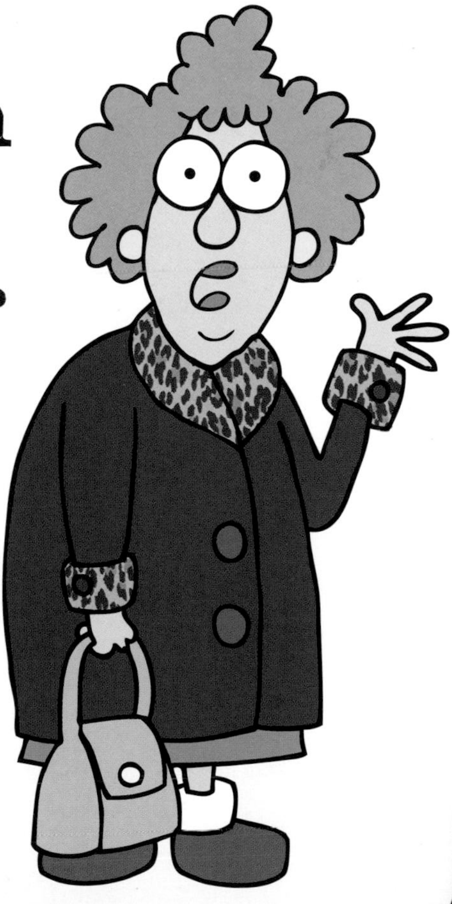

People in glass houses
should not throw
stones
they should throw
parties...
with
firefighter
calendar
boys.

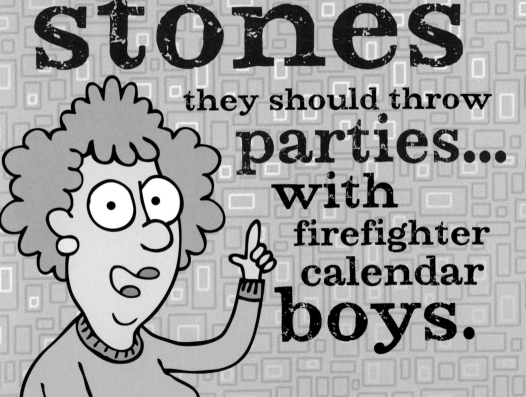

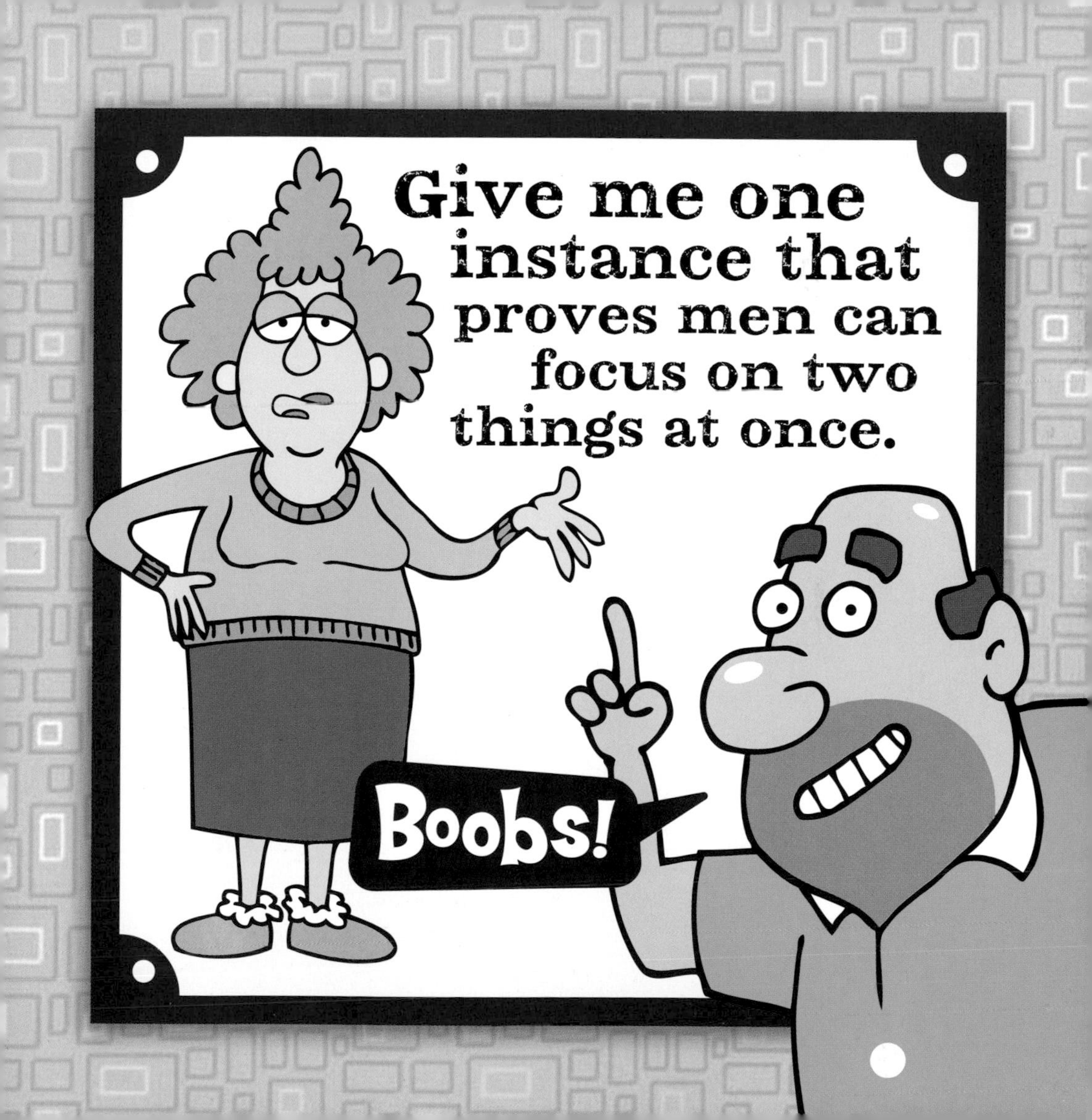
Give me one instance that proves men can focus on two things at once.
Boobs!

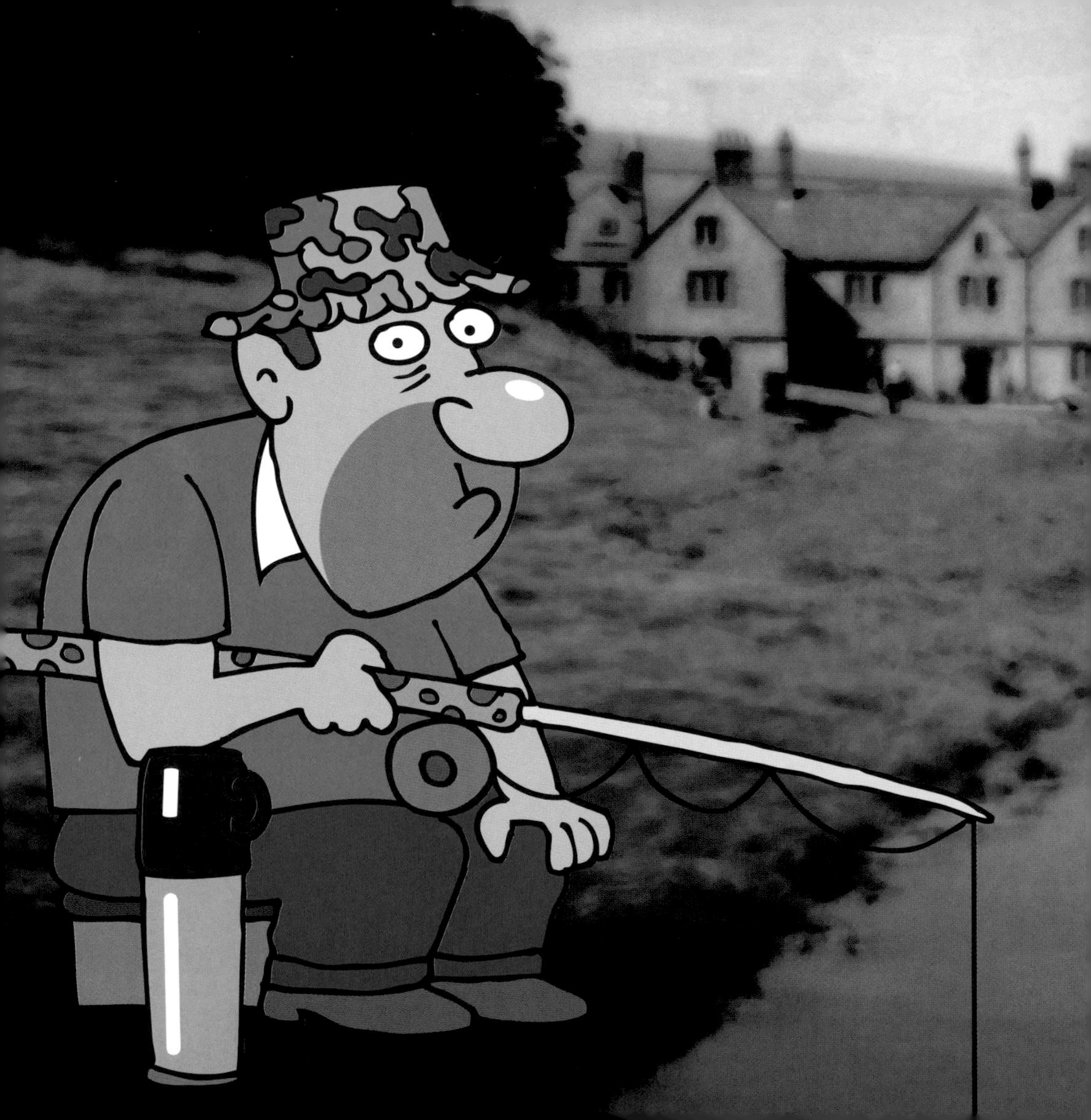

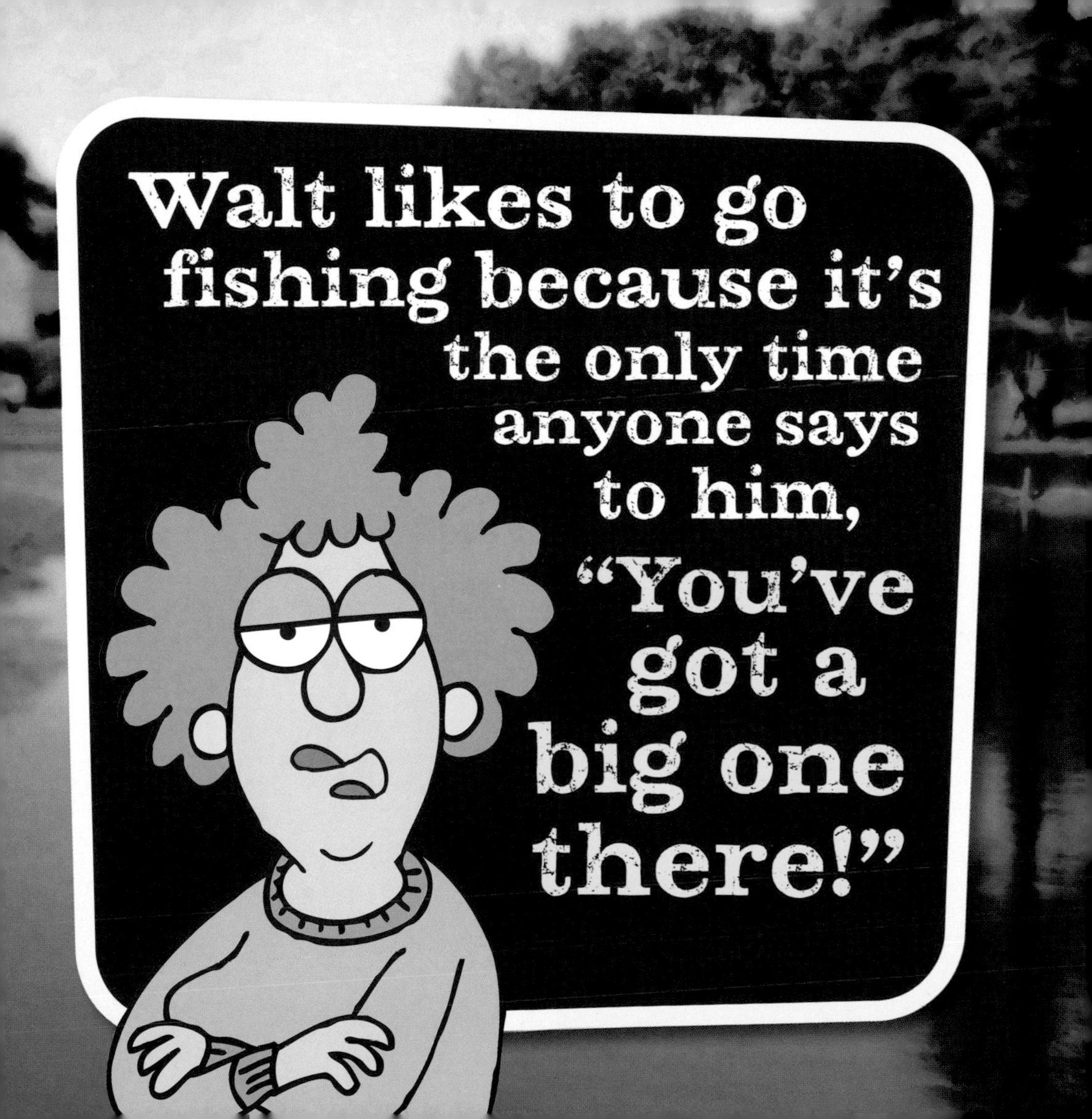
Walt likes to go fishing because it's the only time anyone says to him, "You've got a big one there!"

Men smell funny.

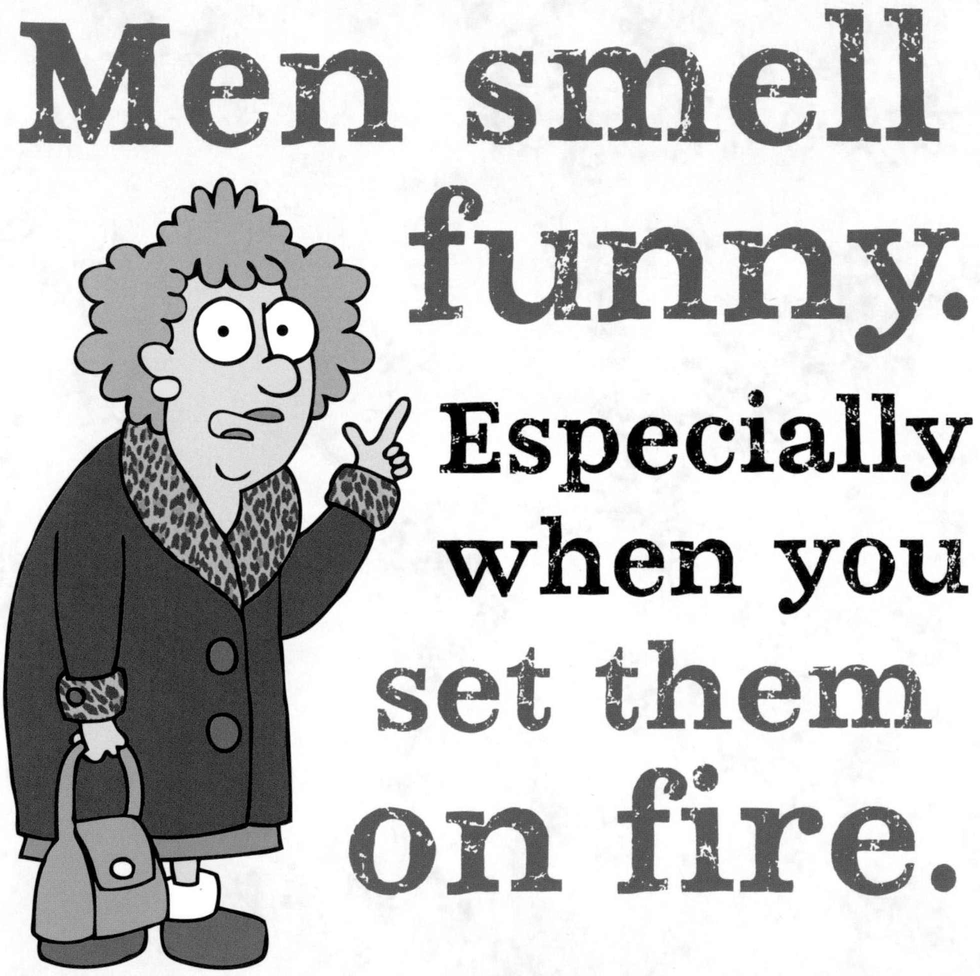

Especially when you set them on fire.

How can a man, who can hit a deer at 200 yards, **keep** missing the **toilet?**

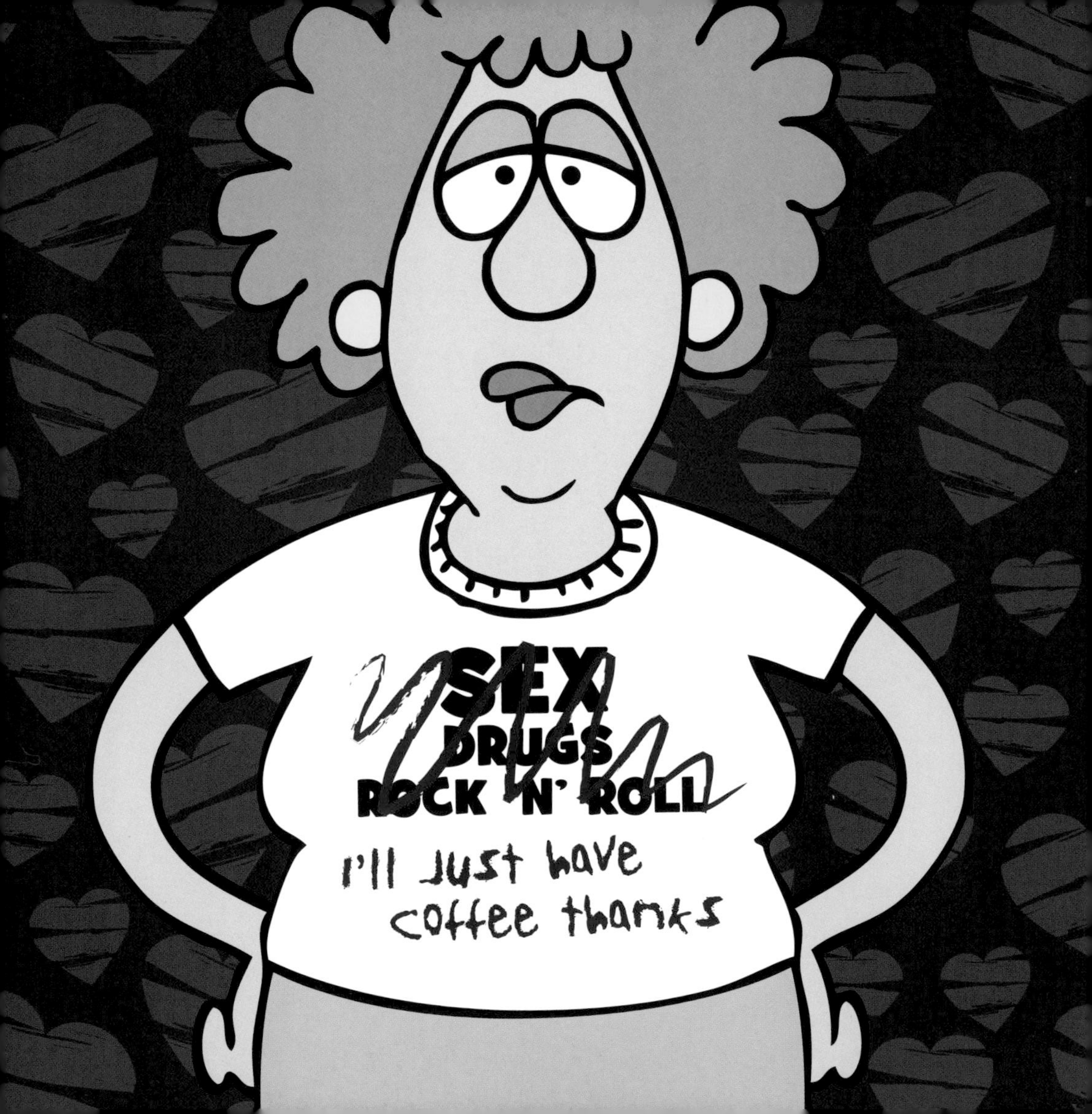
SEX
DRUGS
ROCK 'N' ROLL
I'll just have coffee thanks

I've just finished

50 shades of pink.

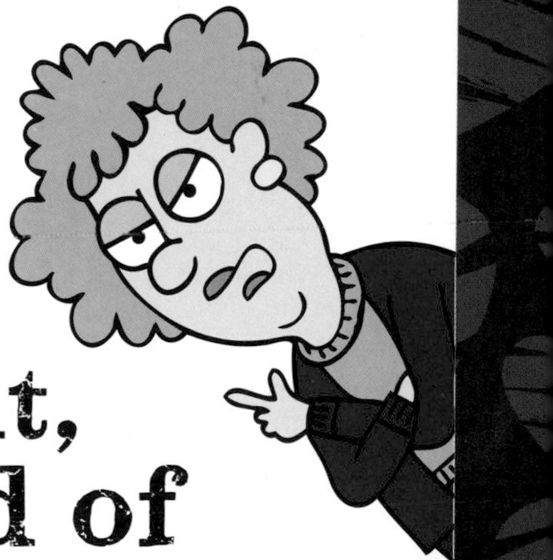

It's a true story about Walt, a load of white washing and an elusive red sock.

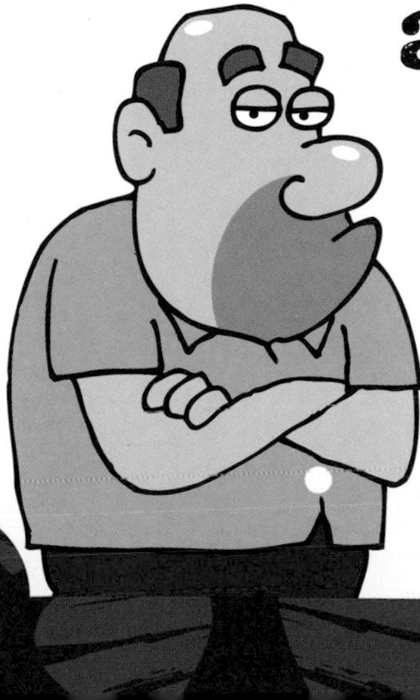

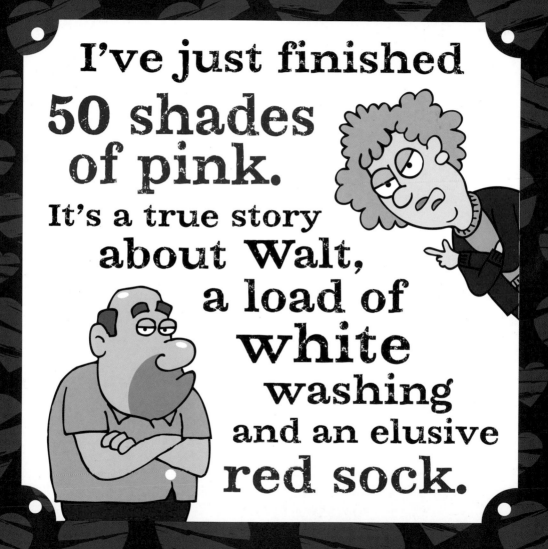

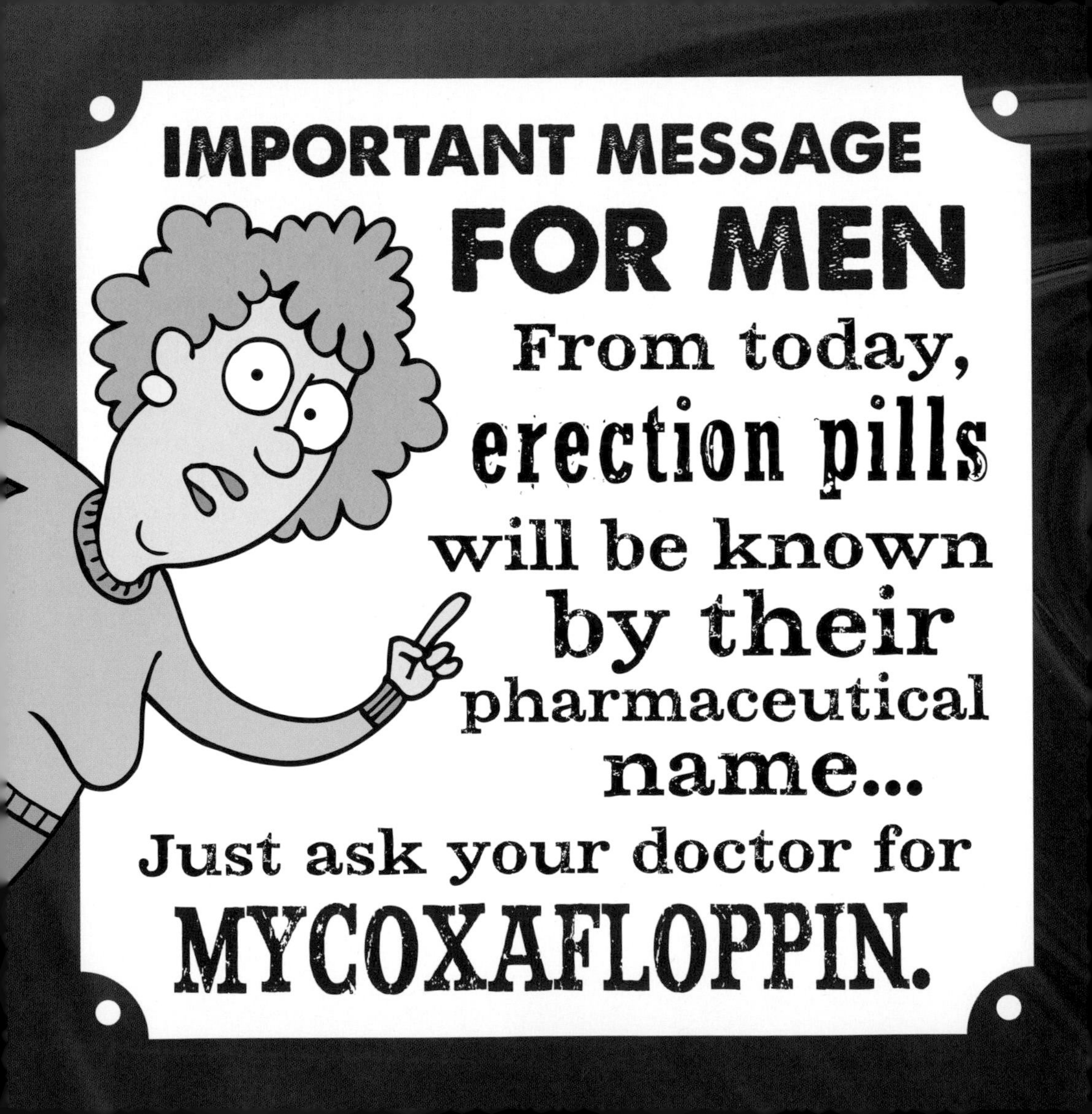
IMPORTANT MESSAGE
FOR MEN
From today,
erection pills
will be known
by their
pharmaceutical
name...
Just ask your doctor for
MYCOXAFLOPPIN.

Hell...
Chocolate
doesn't
ask silly
questions.

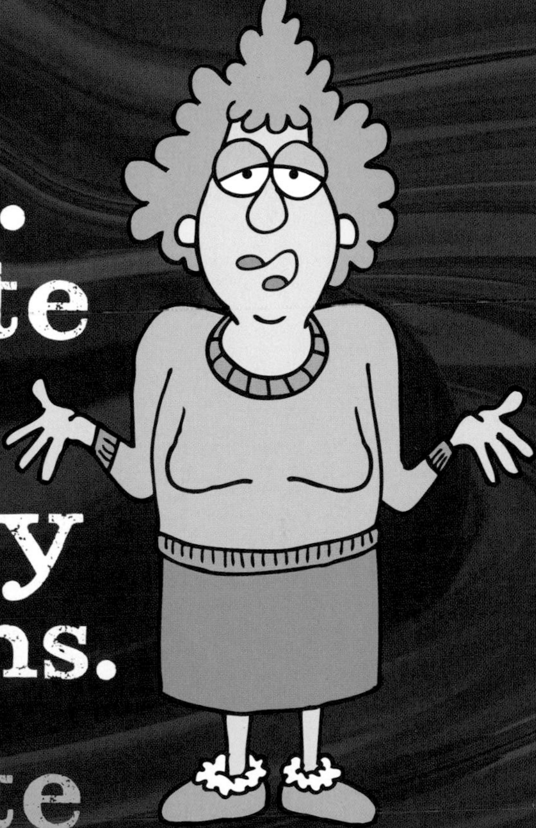

Chocolate
just understands.

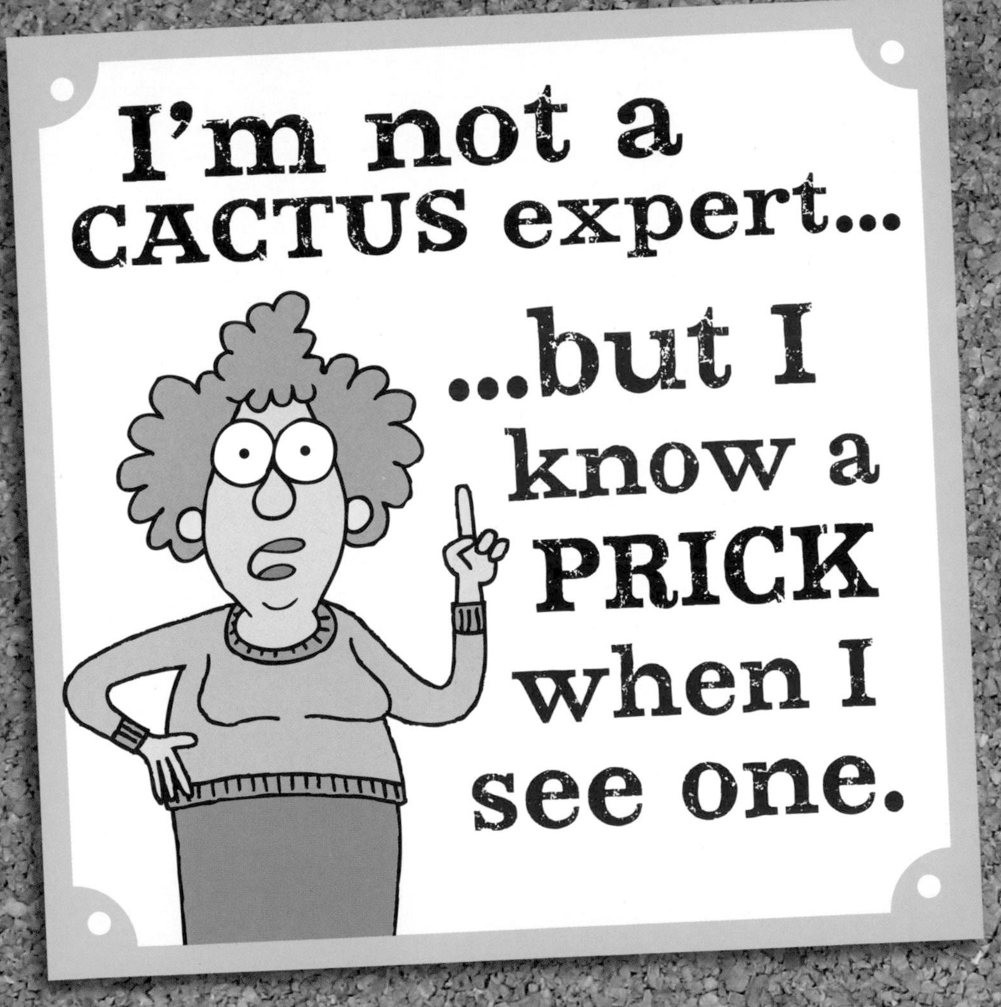
I'm not a
CACTUS expert...
...but I
know a
PRICK
when I
see one.

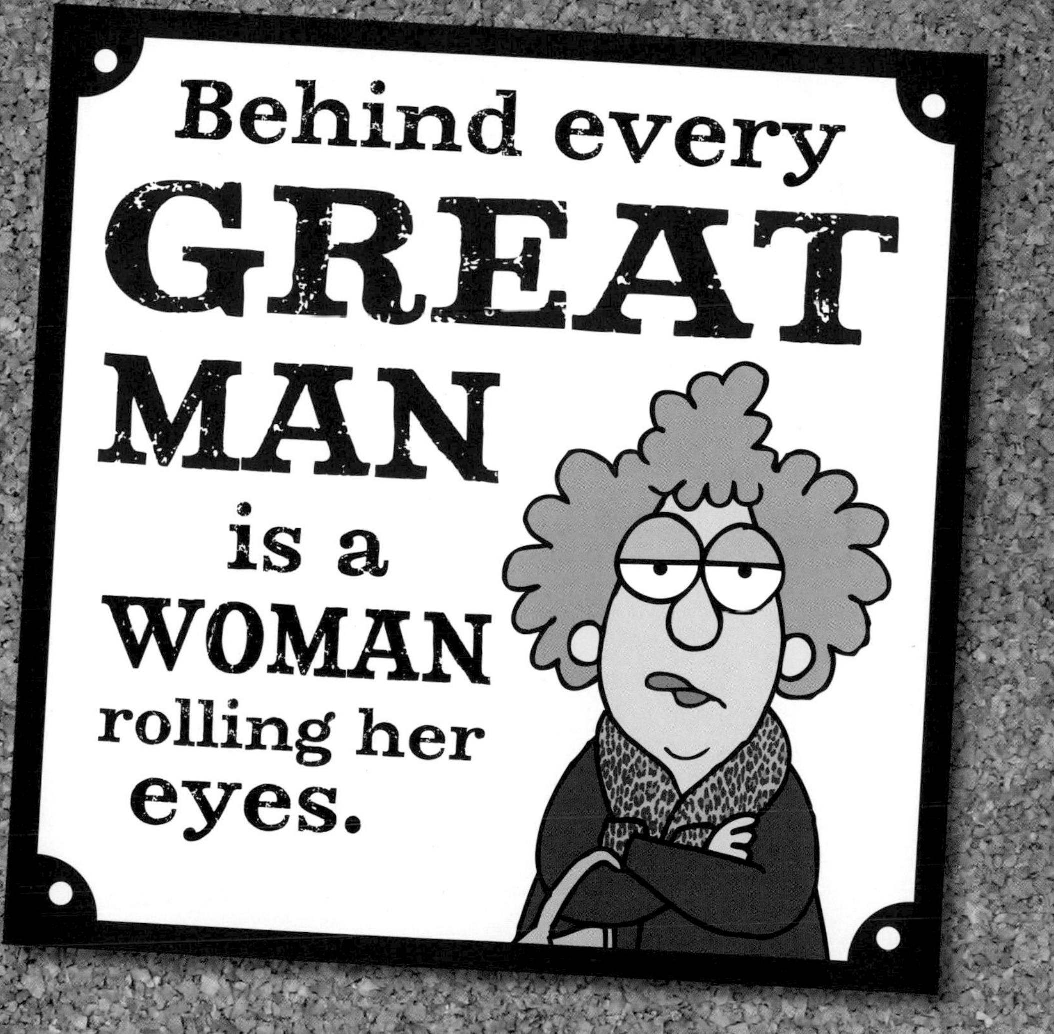
Behind every
GREAT
MAN
is a
WOMAN
rolling her
eyes.

Never run after
a bus or
a man.

There'll
always
be
another.

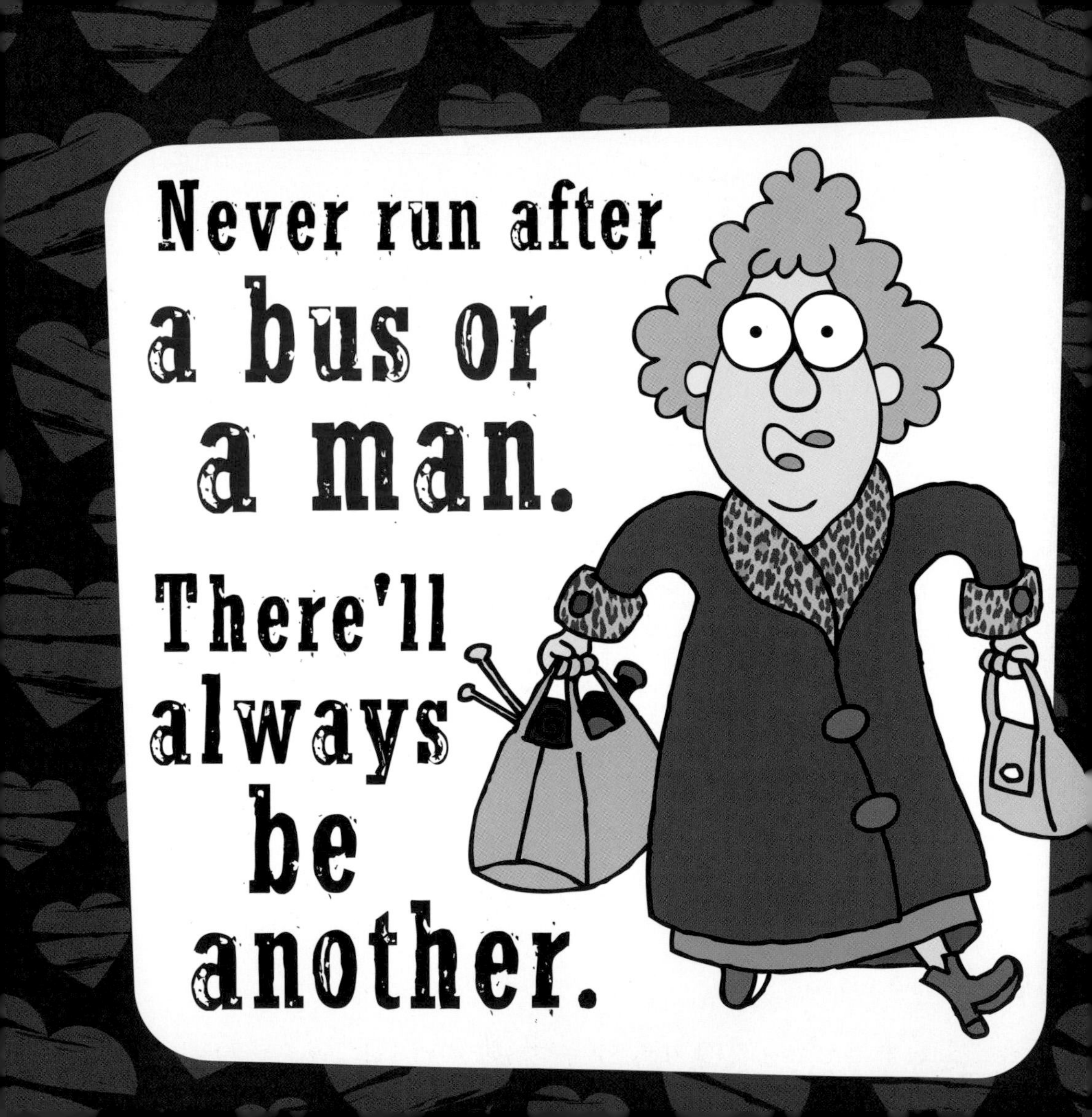

My **husband** thinks I'm **crazy** ...but I'm not the one who married **me!**

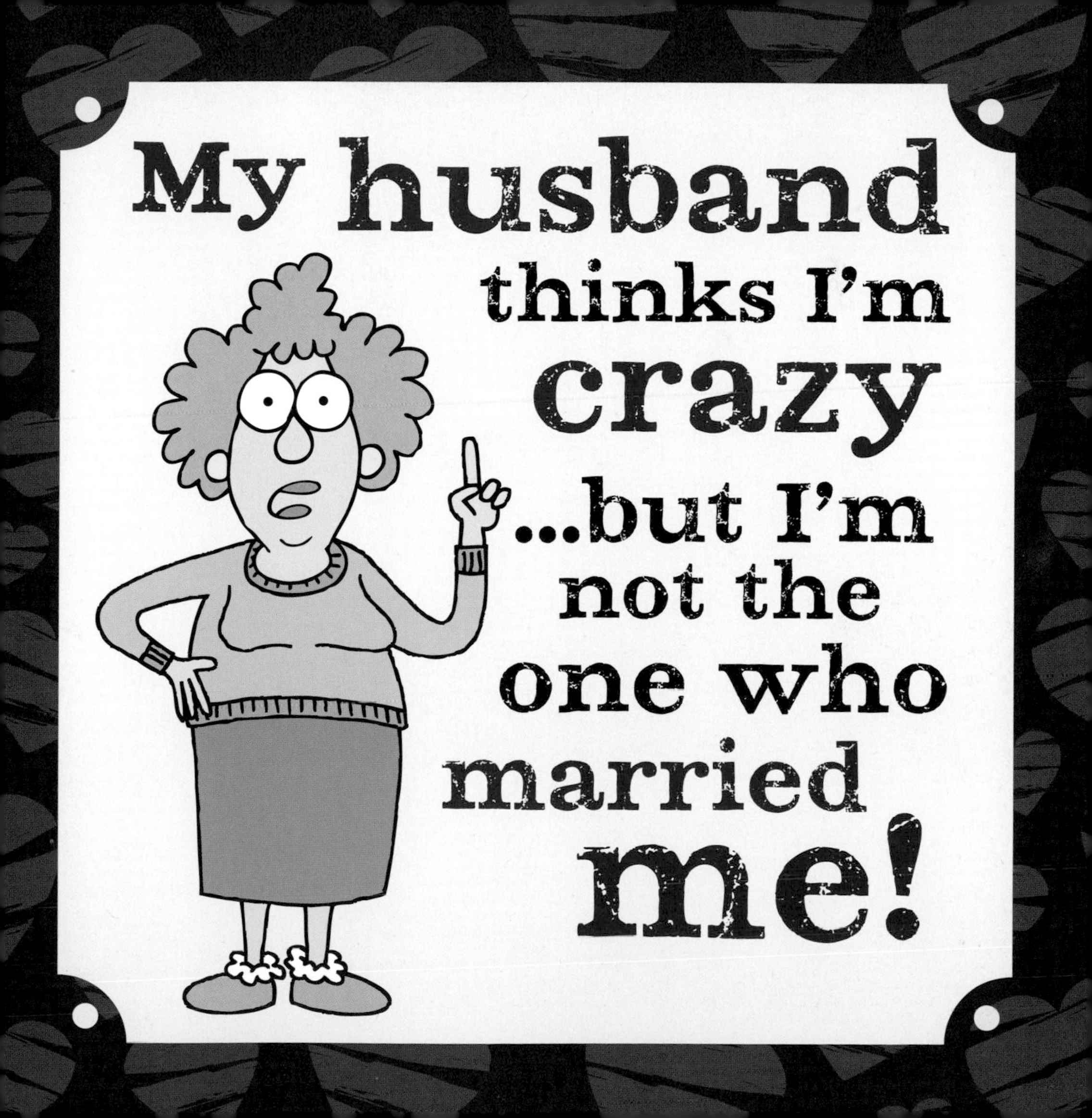

If you think women are the **weaker sex,** try pulling the bed sheets back to your side.

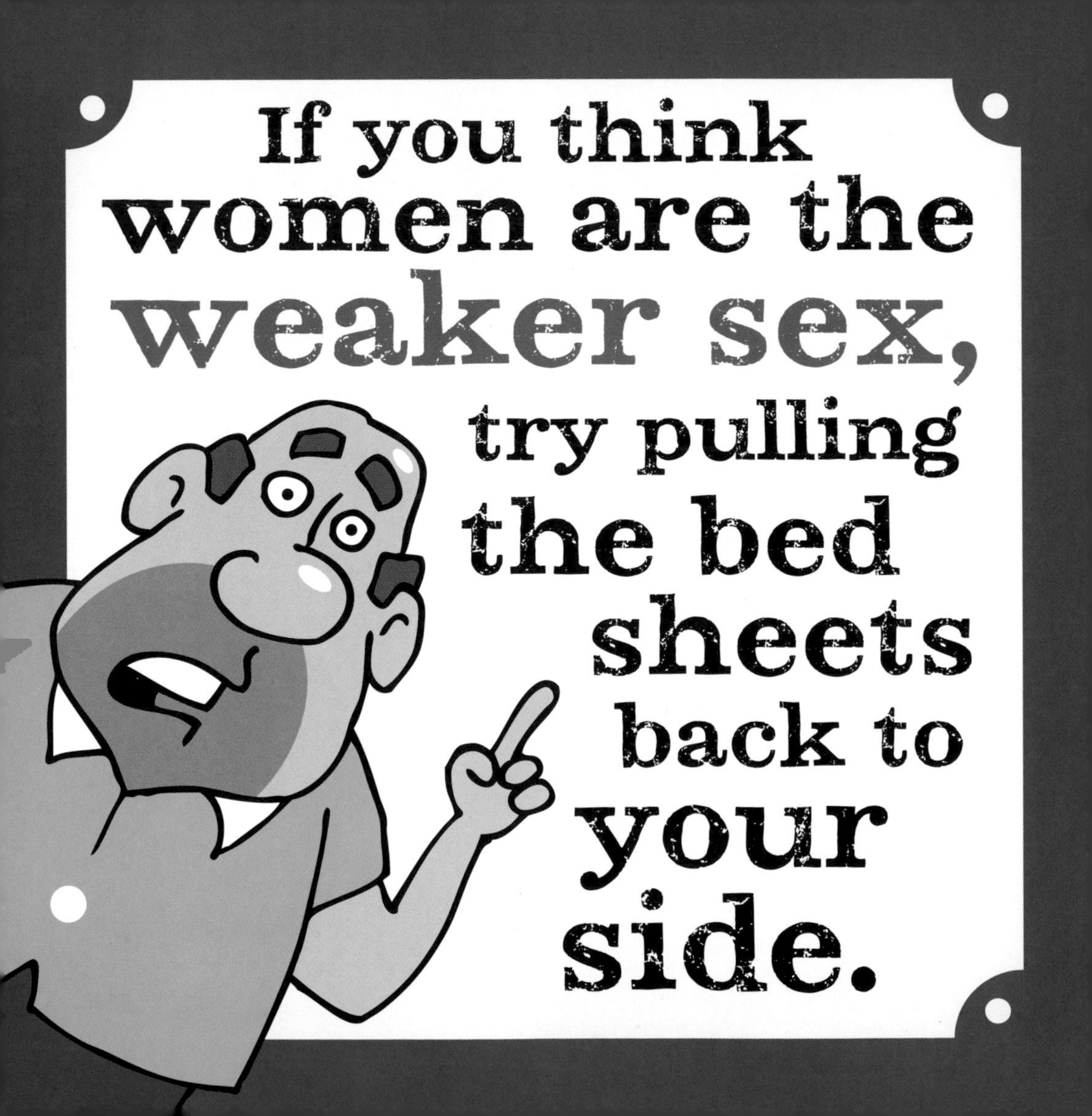

If women belong in the KITCHEN then surely MEN belong in the GARAGE with all the other TOOLS.

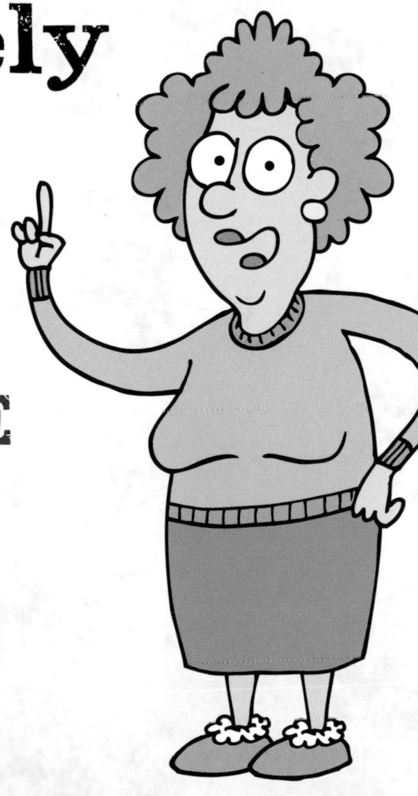

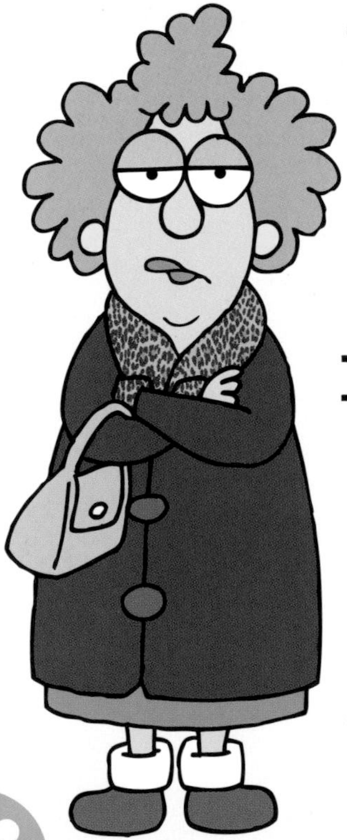

I understand that your **heart** is in the right place. Unfortunately, your head is up your ass.

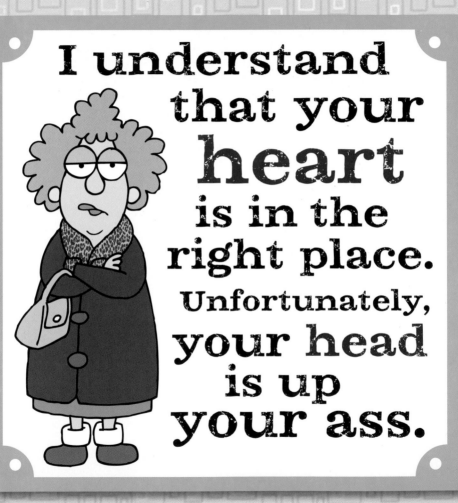

MY LIFE IS LIKE A ROMANTIC COMEDY...
WITHOUT THE
ROMANCE.
AT LEAST MY JOKES ARE FUNNY!

So apparently a man who treats his woman like a princess is proof that he has been raised by a queen... or in my Walt's case, the jester.

Saying that, had my fair share of losers, but, hey, at least my Prince Charming got here in the end, he just rode in on a freakin' turtle instead of a horse, that's all.

So read on for my advice on moronic men and ridiculous relationships.

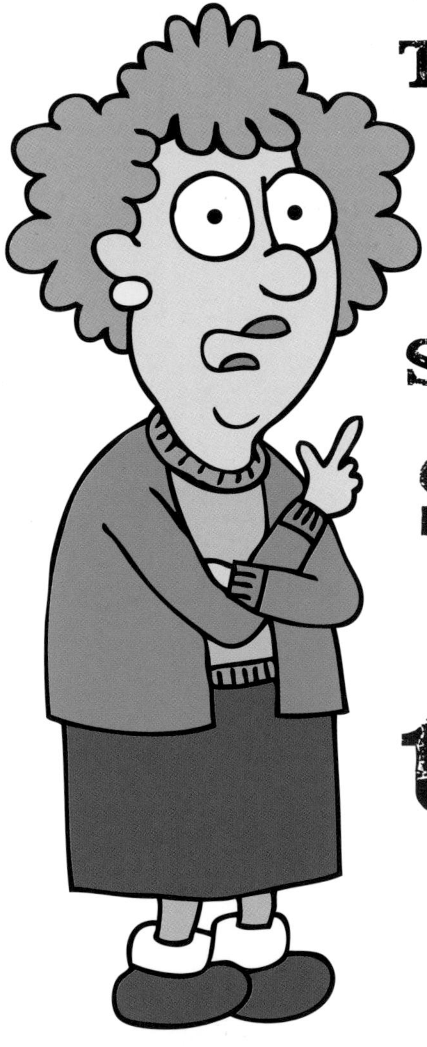

The best way to get a man to do something?

Suggest he's too old for it.

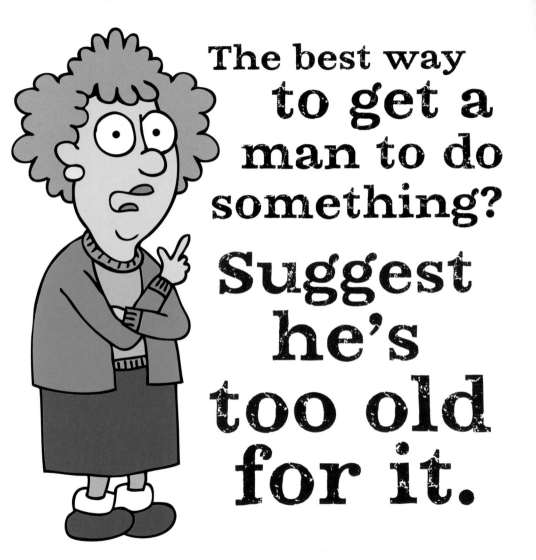

My husband is a
wonderful
provider.

He provides
me with...
ulcers,
headaches,
high blood
pressure...

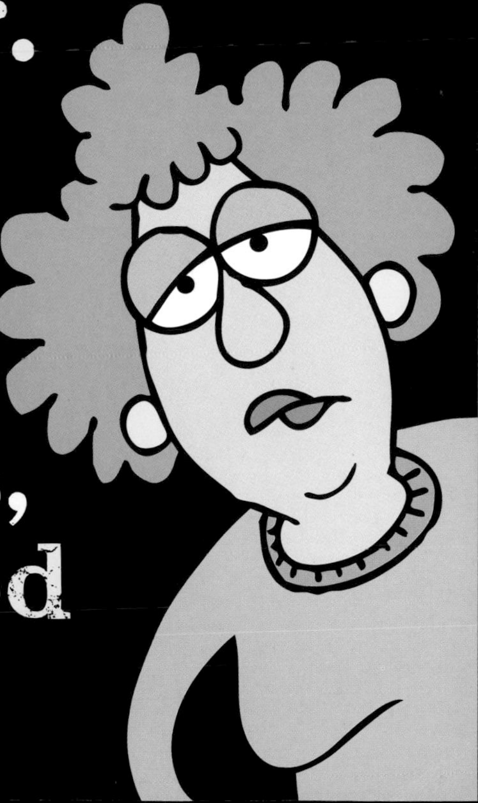

Walt said the **spark** between us had gone, so I tasered him. I'll ask him again when he wakes up.

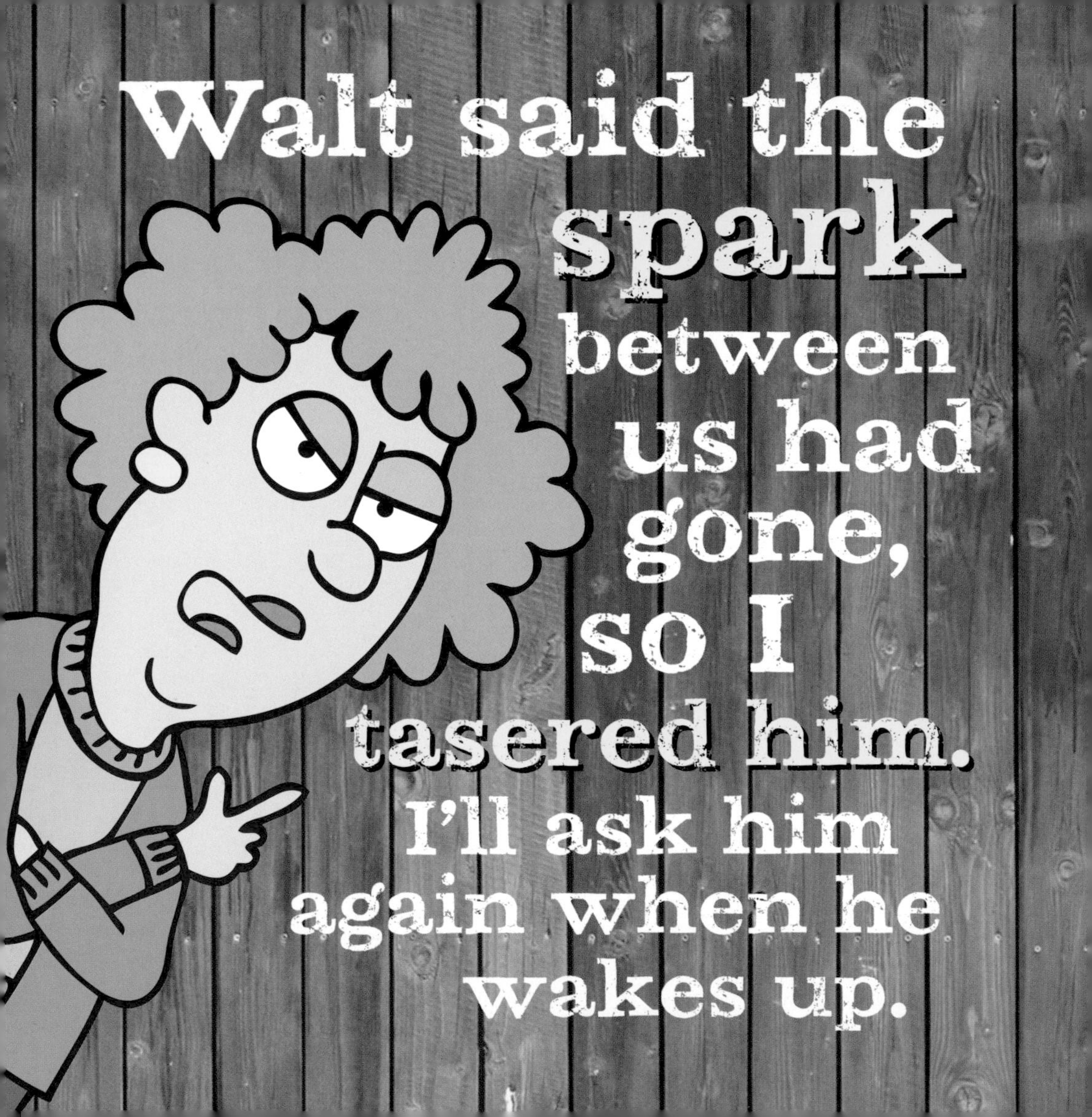

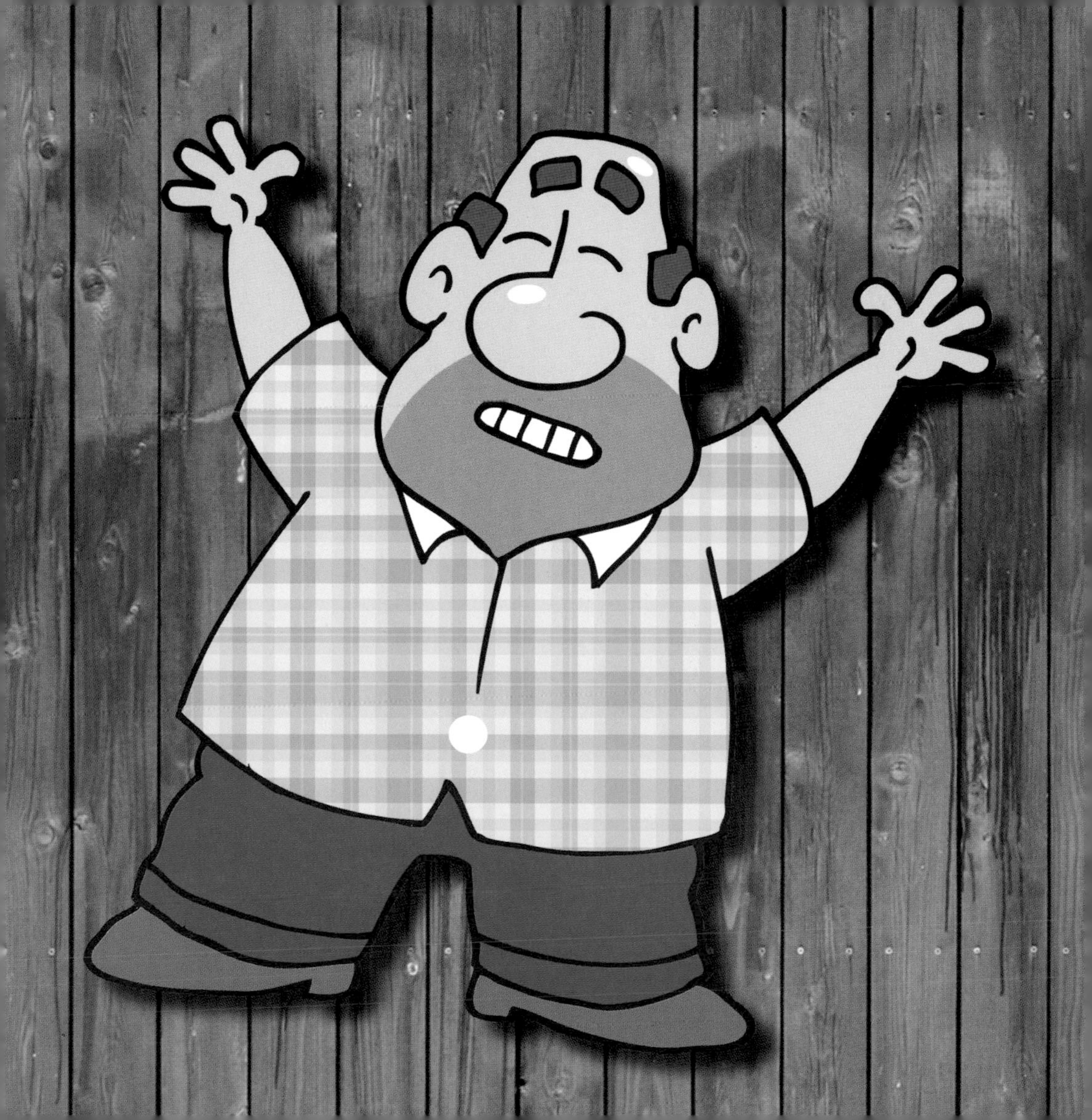

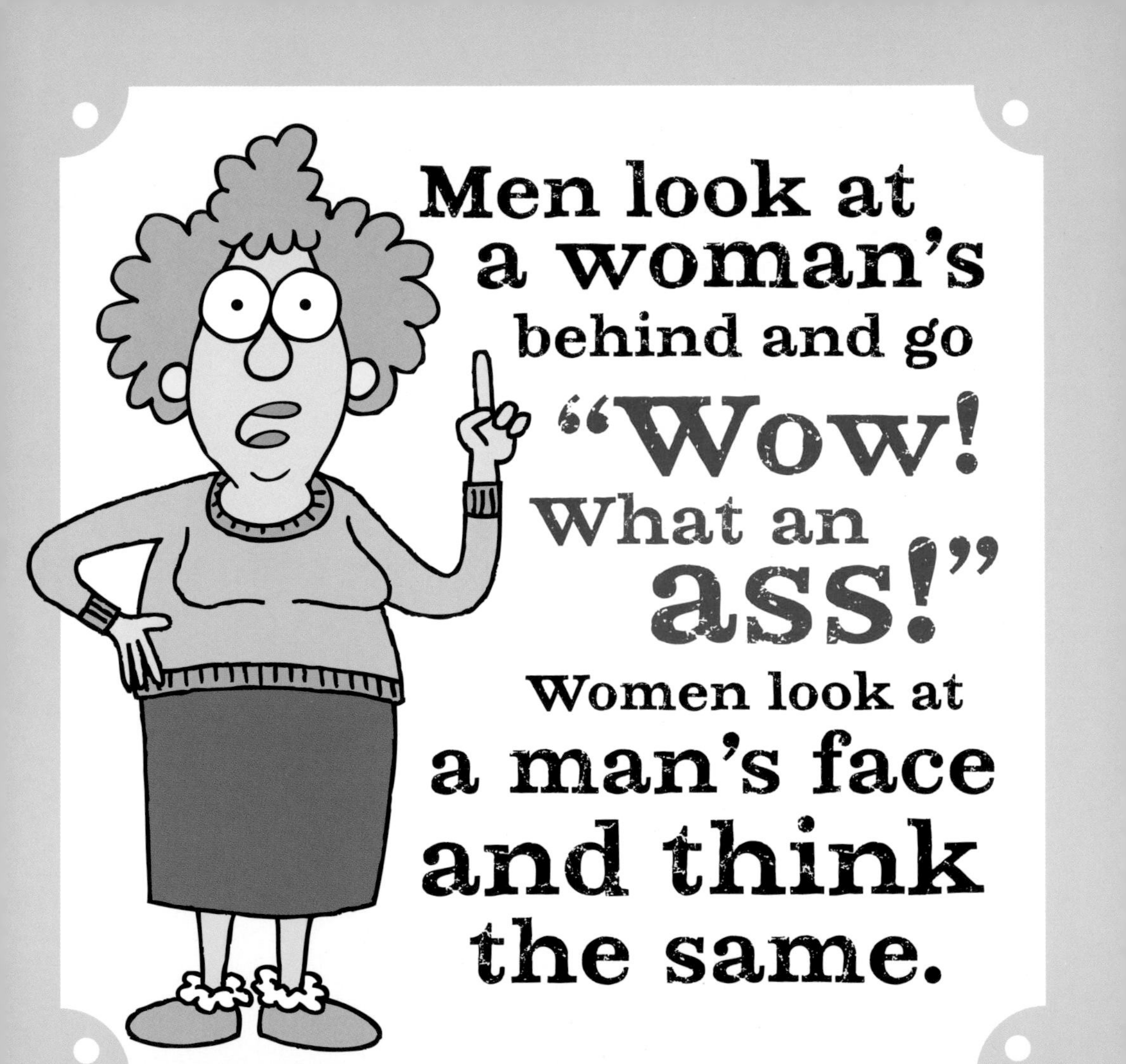

Men look at
a woman's
behind and go
"Wow!
What an
ass!"
Women look at
a man's face
and think
the same.

I've been having problems with **nuisance** phone calls lately.

The most common one seems to be, "You said you'd be home from shopping 3 hours ago!"

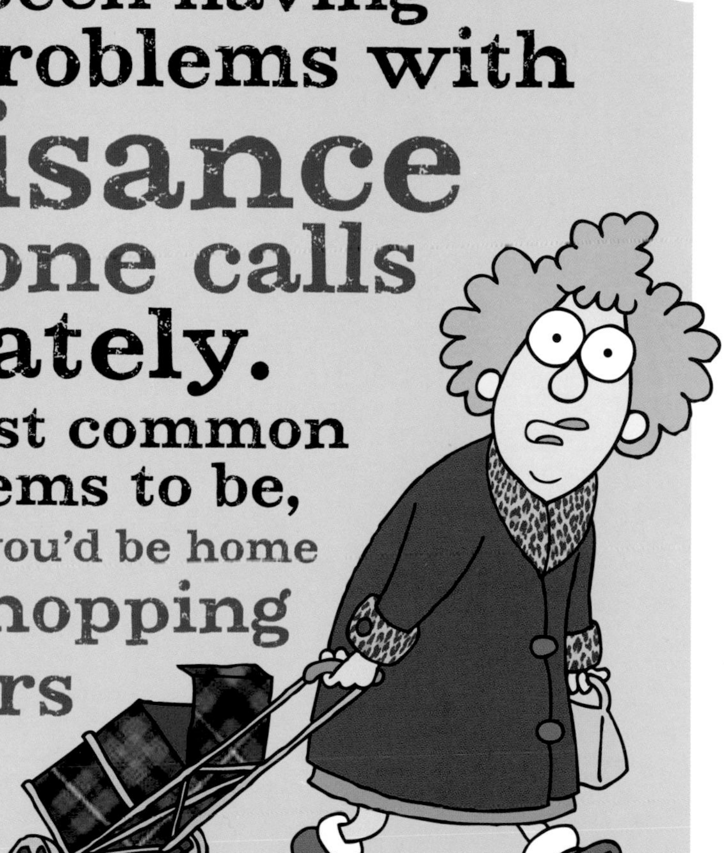

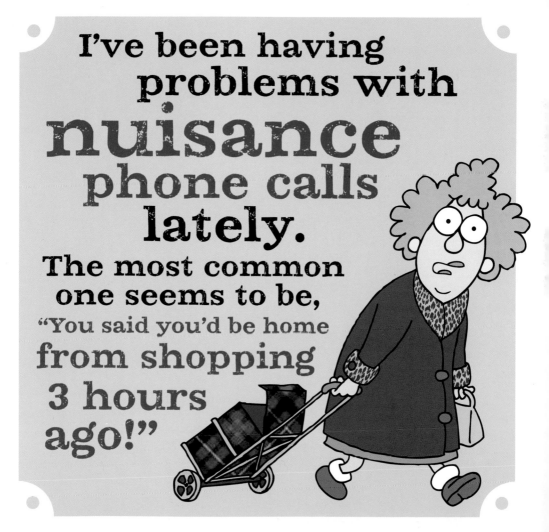

I've always wanted to know how long **forever** was—and by looking at some people's **Facebook** relationships, it appears to be around **2 to 4 weeks.**

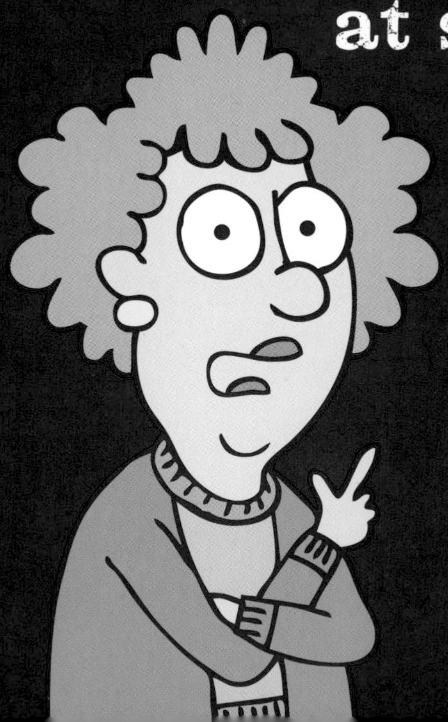

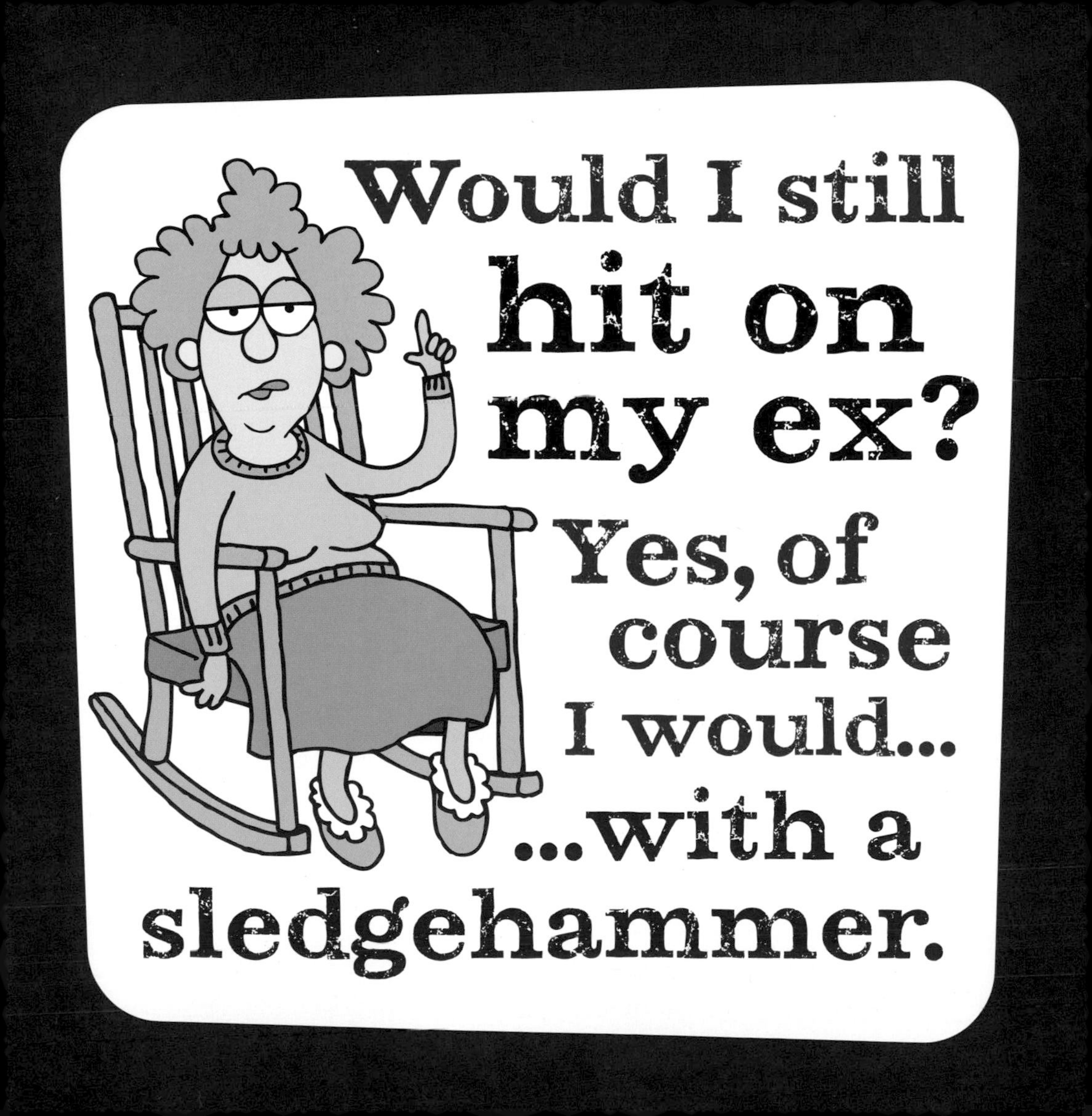

Would I still hit on my ex? Yes, of course I would... ...with a sledgehammer.

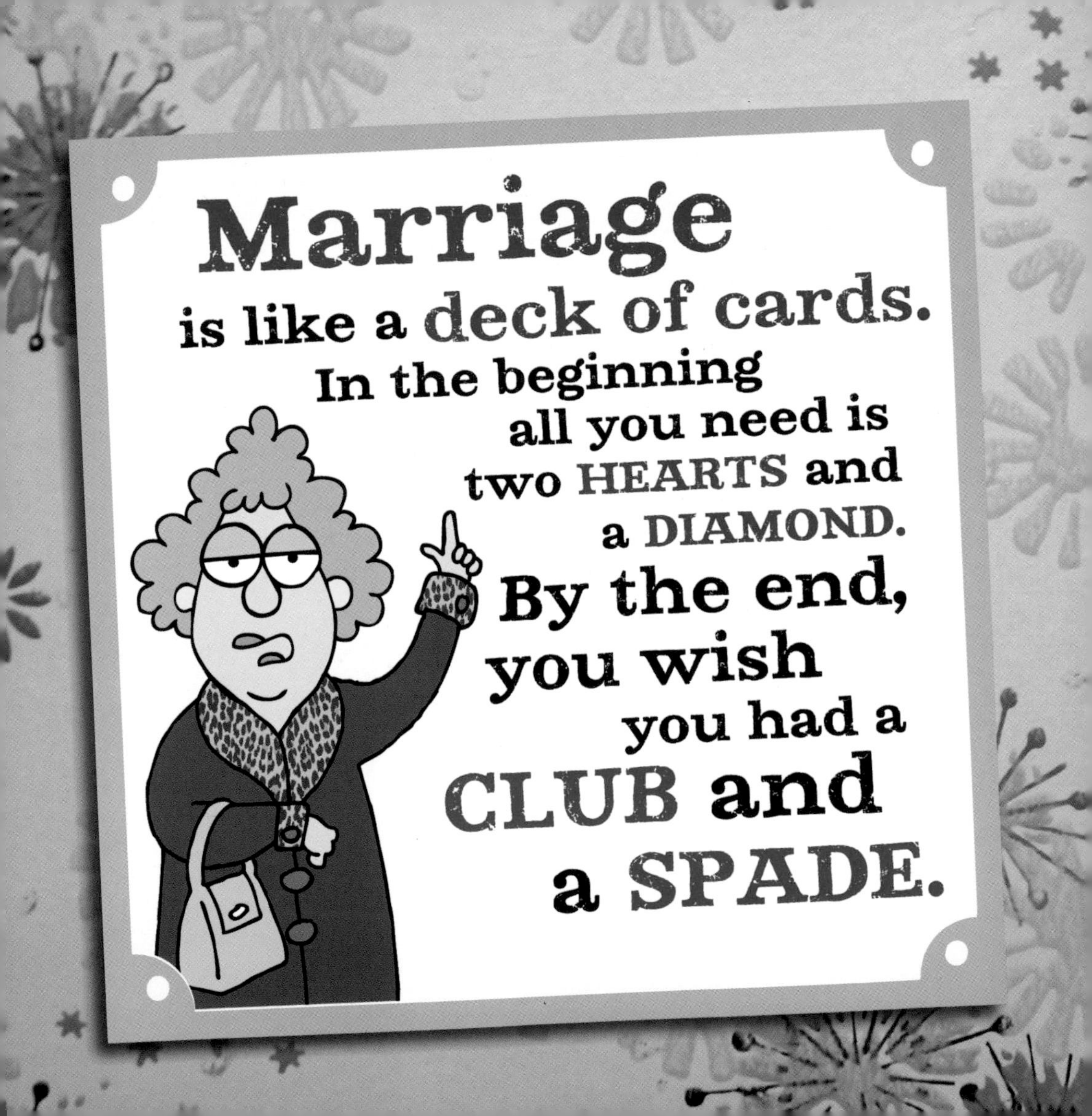
Marriage
is like a deck of cards.
In the beginning
all you need is
two HEARTS and
a DIAMOND.
By the end,
you wish
you had a
CLUB and
a SPADE.

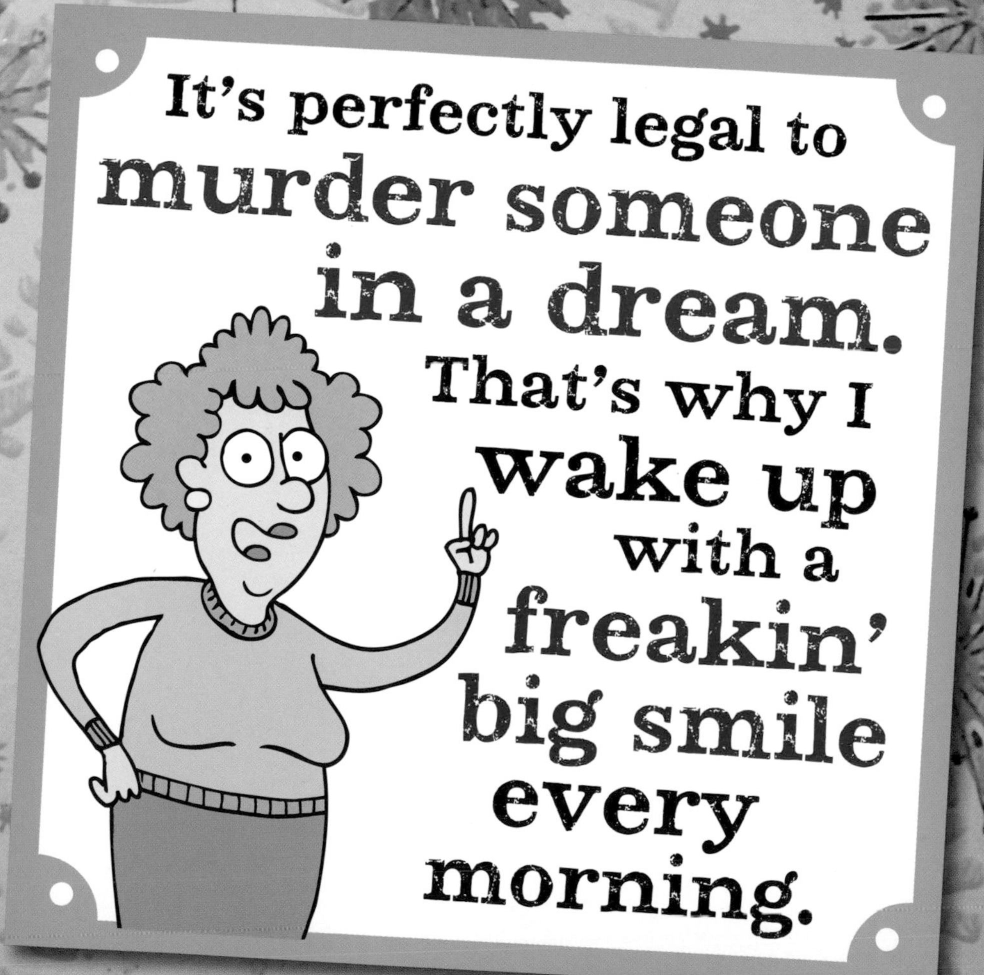
It's perfectly legal to
murder someone
in a dream.
That's why I
wake up
with a
freakin'
big smile
every
morning.

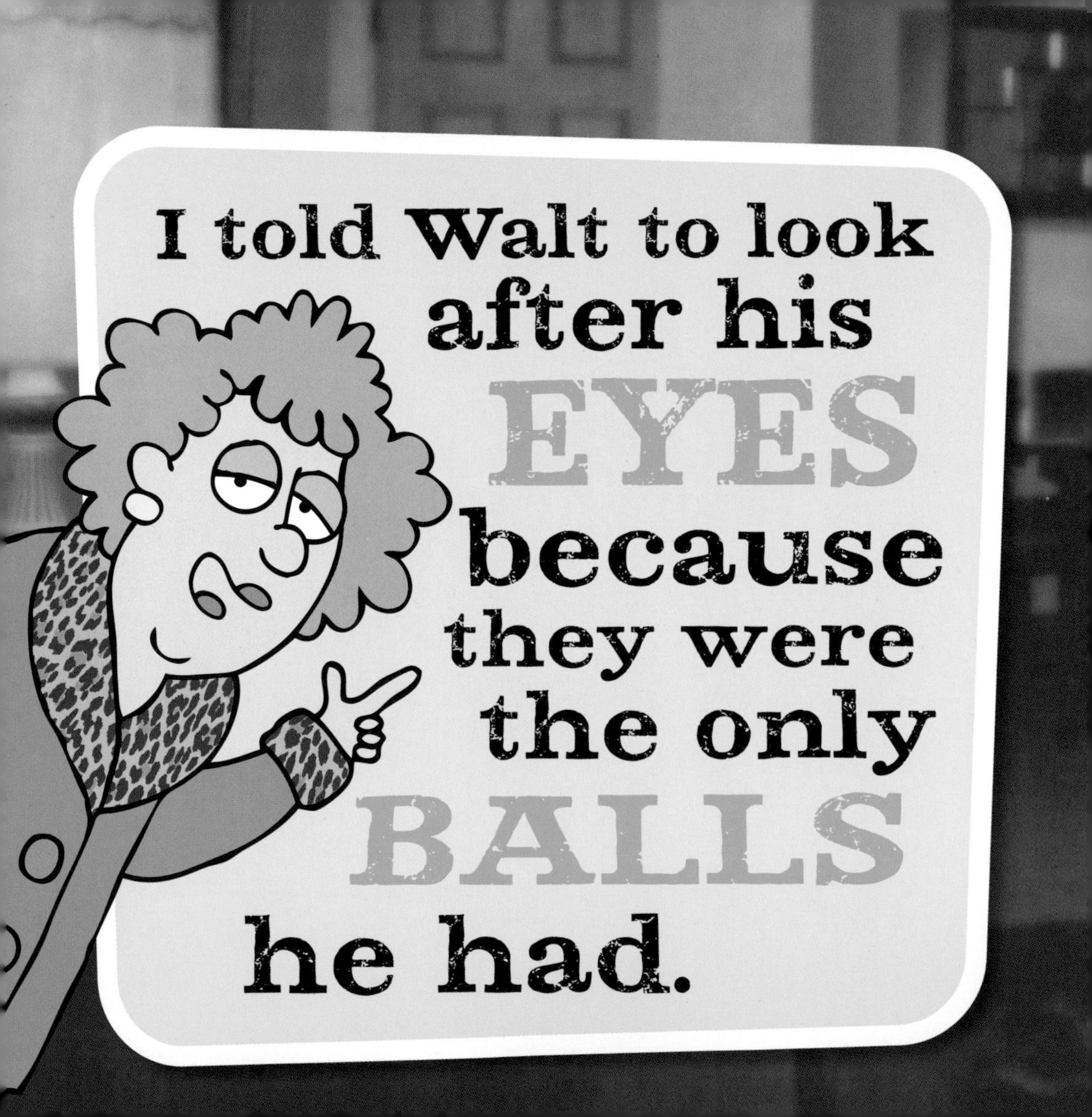
I told Walt to look after his EYES because they were the only BALLS he had.

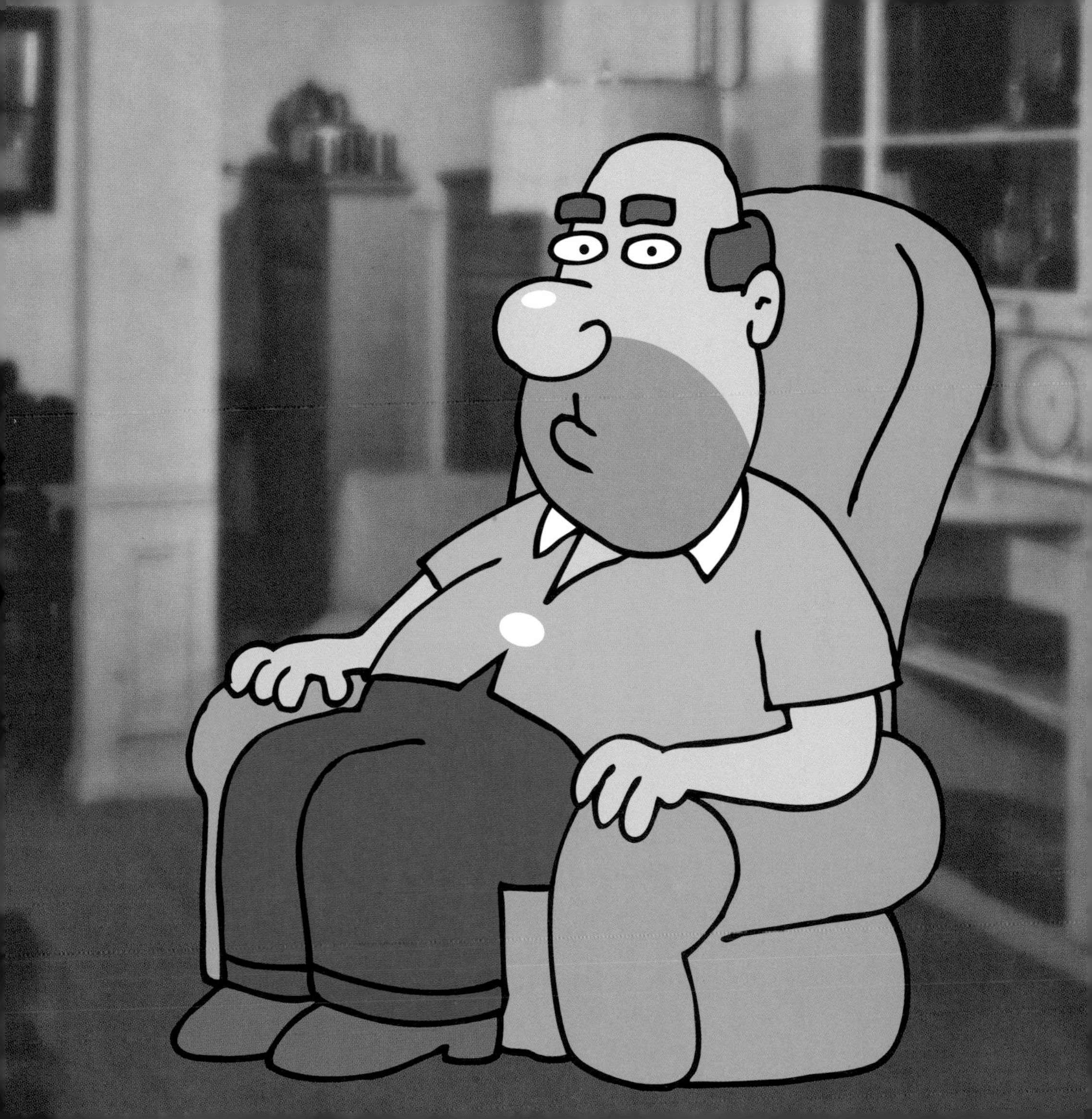

While lying in bed with my husband last night, he asked me what I'd most like to do with his body....

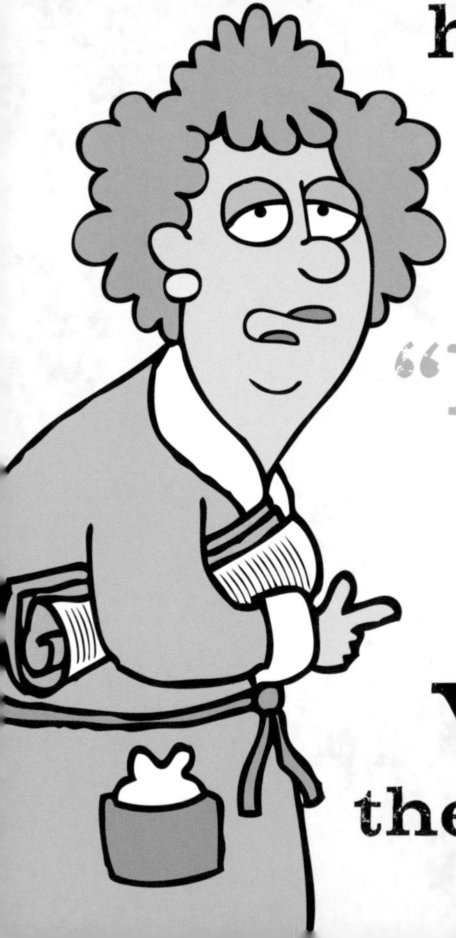

"IDENTIFY IT" apparently wasn't the right answer.

Some people need their

beauty sleep...

...but my ex-husband's new woman,

hell—

she needs to hibernate.

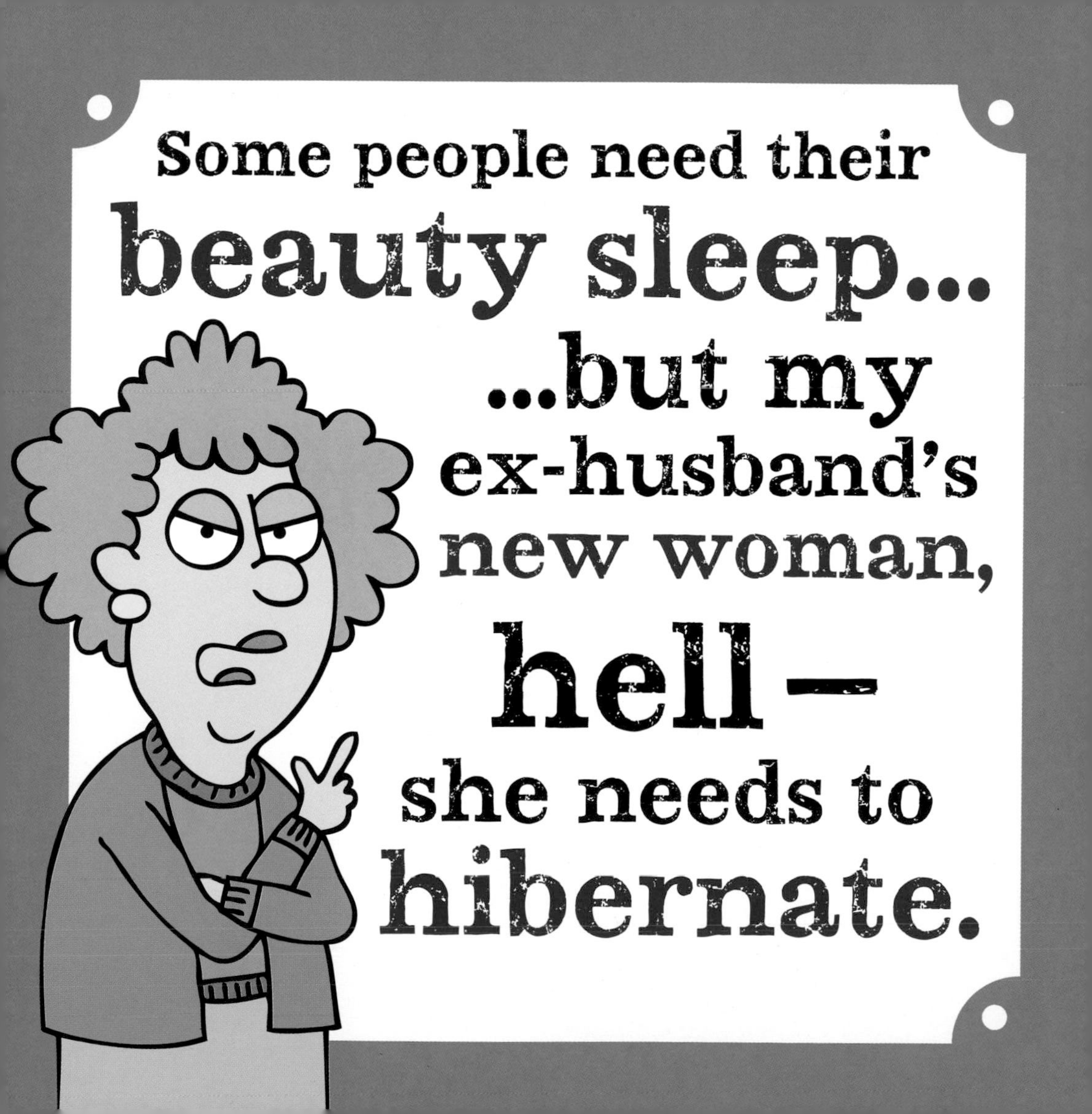

Apparently
Man-Flu
is more
painful than
childbirth.
This is an
irrefutable
scientific fact.*

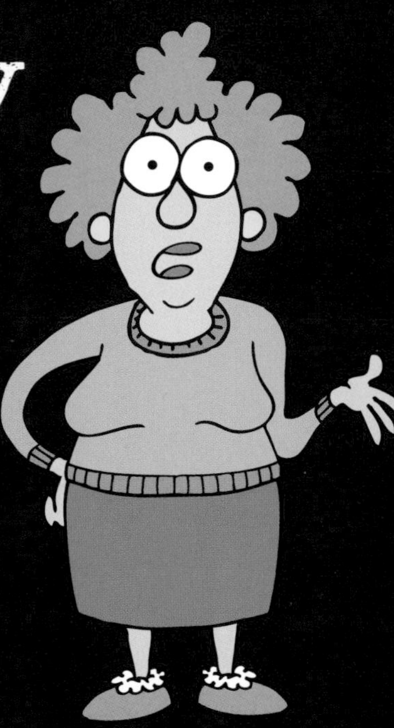

*(Based on a survey of over 100,000 men.)

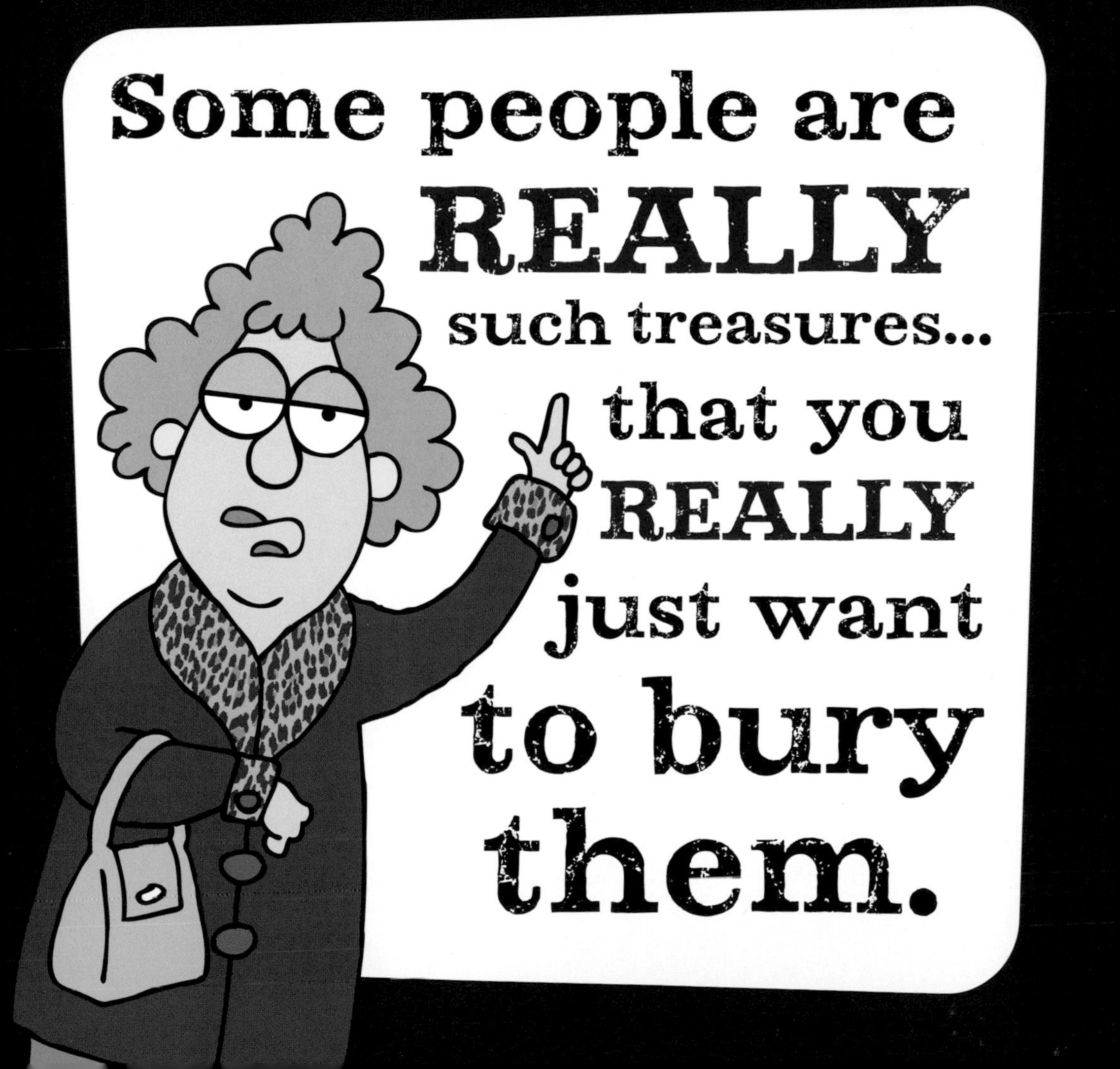
Some people are
REALLY
such treasures...
that you
REALLY
just want
to bury
them.

The most used sexual position for married couples is doggie style. The husband sits up and begs ...and the wife rolls over and plays dead.

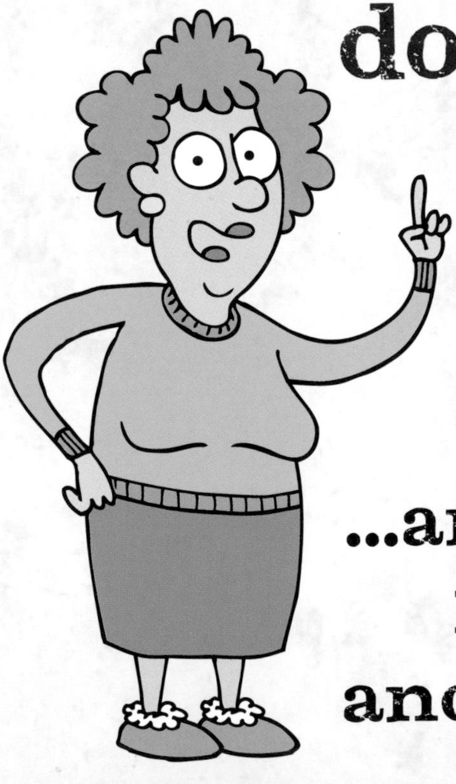

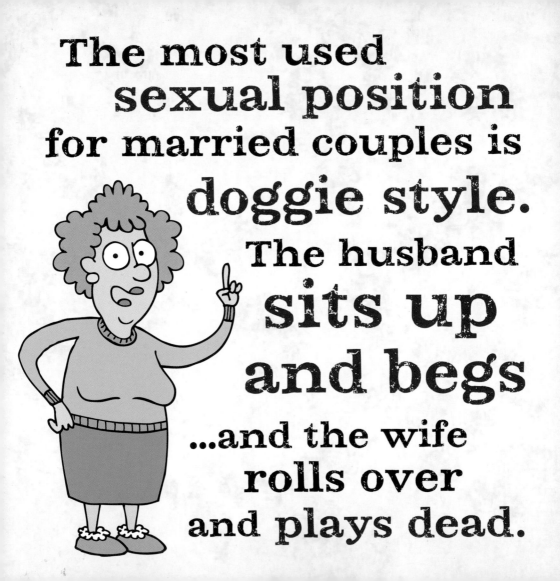

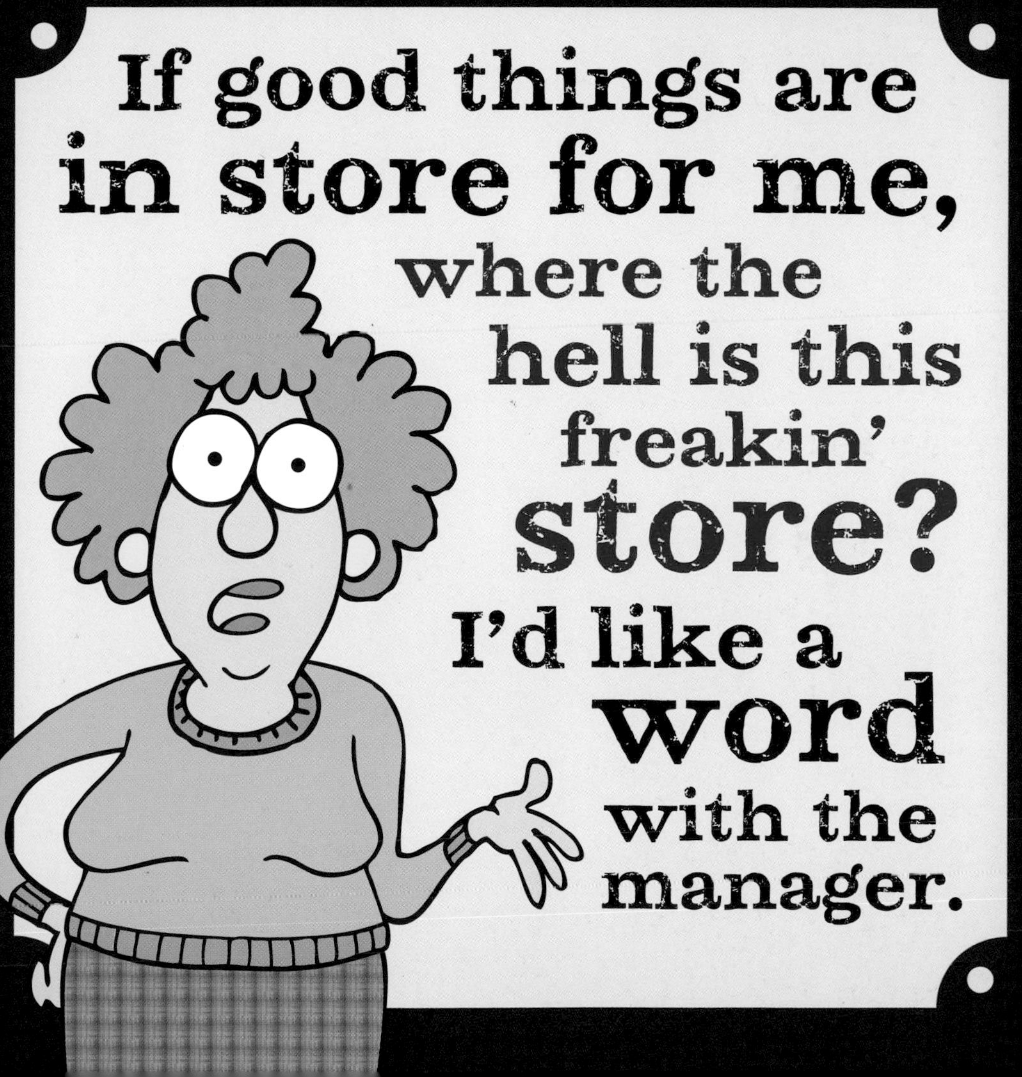
If good things are in store for me, where the hell is this freakin' store? I'd like a word with the manager.

A scientific report has found out why female spiders eat their mates.

It turns out that male spiders freakin' deserve it.

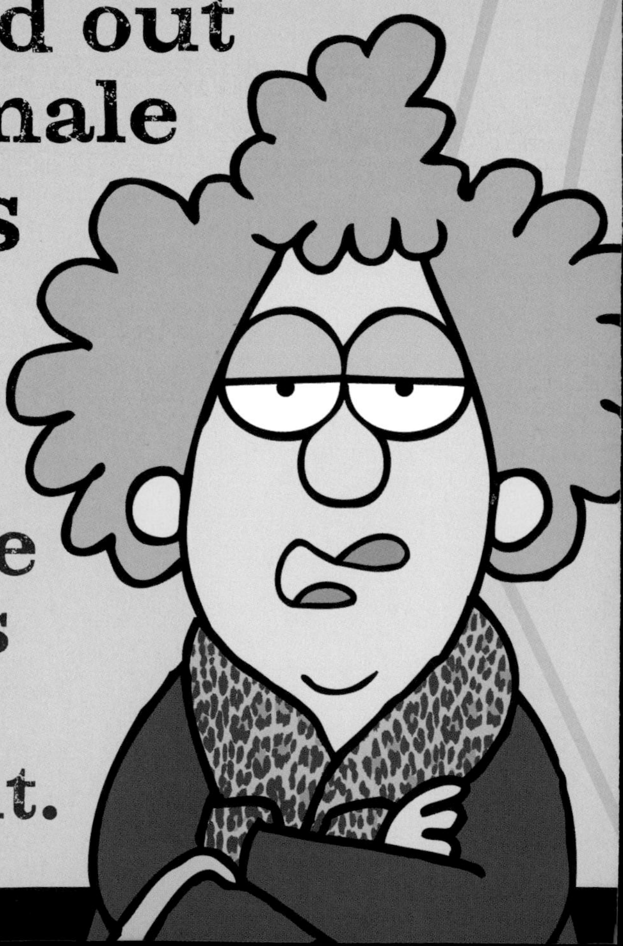

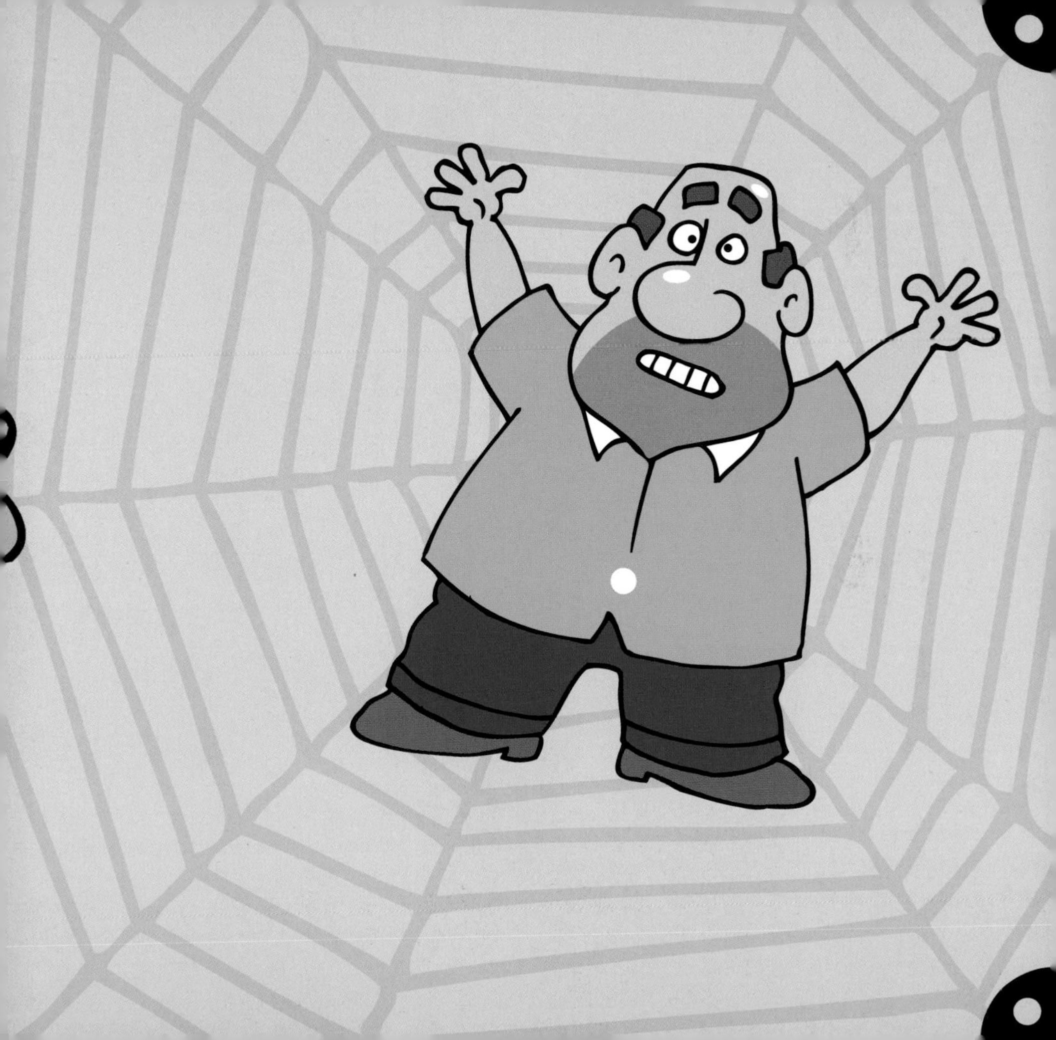

A friend of mine confused her Valium with her birth control pills. She has 14 kids but doesn't really care.

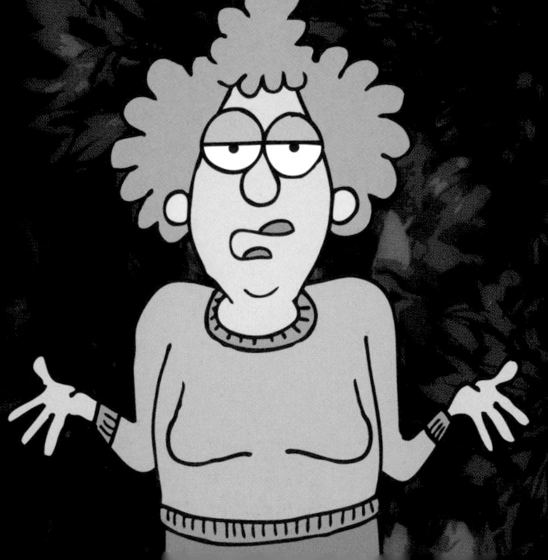

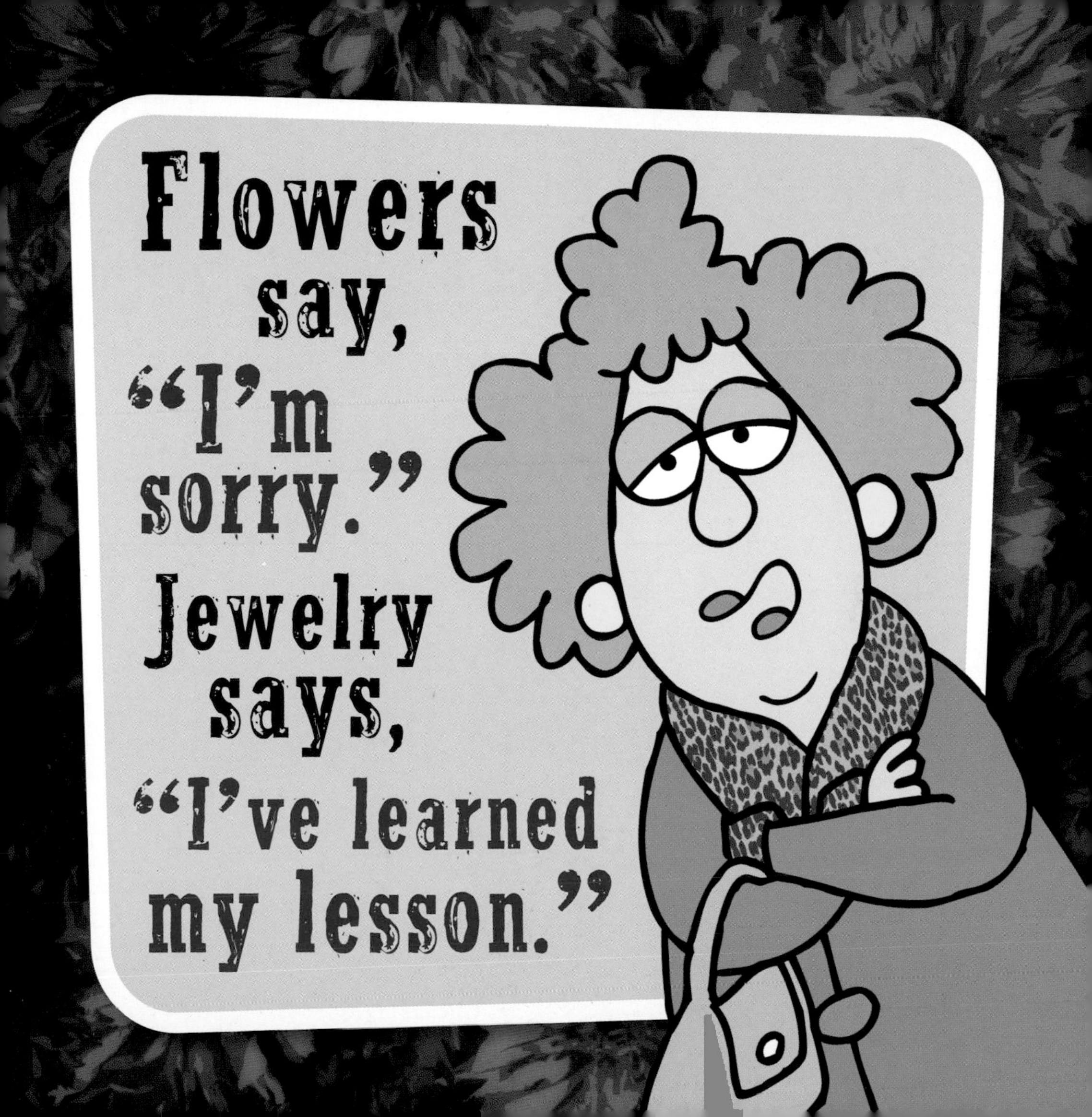
Flowers say, "I'm sorry."
Jewelry says, "I've learned my lesson."

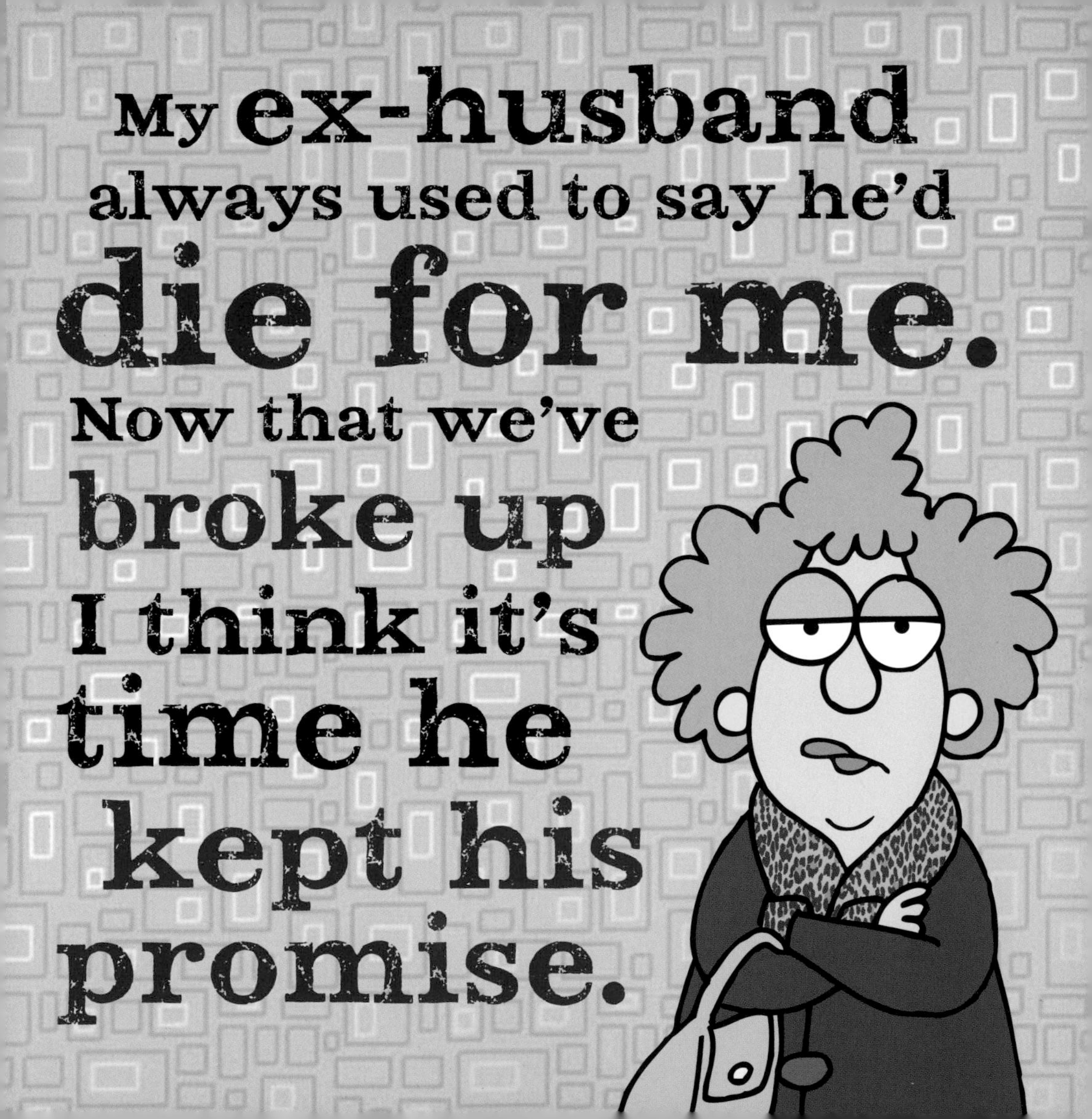
My ex-husband always used to say he'd die for me. Now that we've broke up I think it's time he kept his promise.

If I was single, I'd avoid
online dating sites
because they match you up
with someone
who is
similar to
yourself
and I
don't want to
go out with
a weirdo.

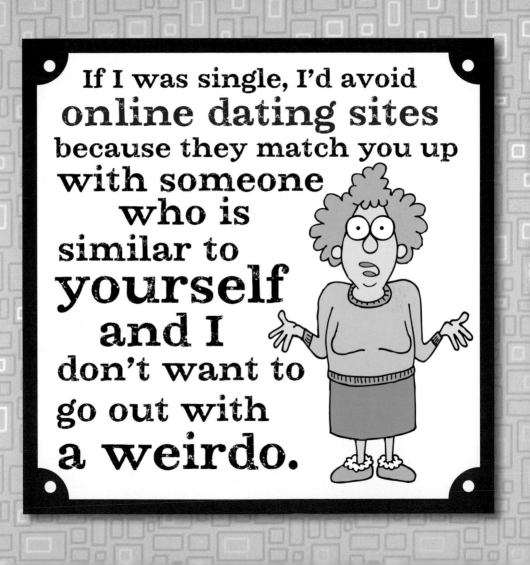

Aunty Acid left a note on the fridge—

"It's not working. I can't take it anymore. I'm going to my sister's."

I opened the fridge, the light came on, the beer was cold...

What the hell is she talking about?

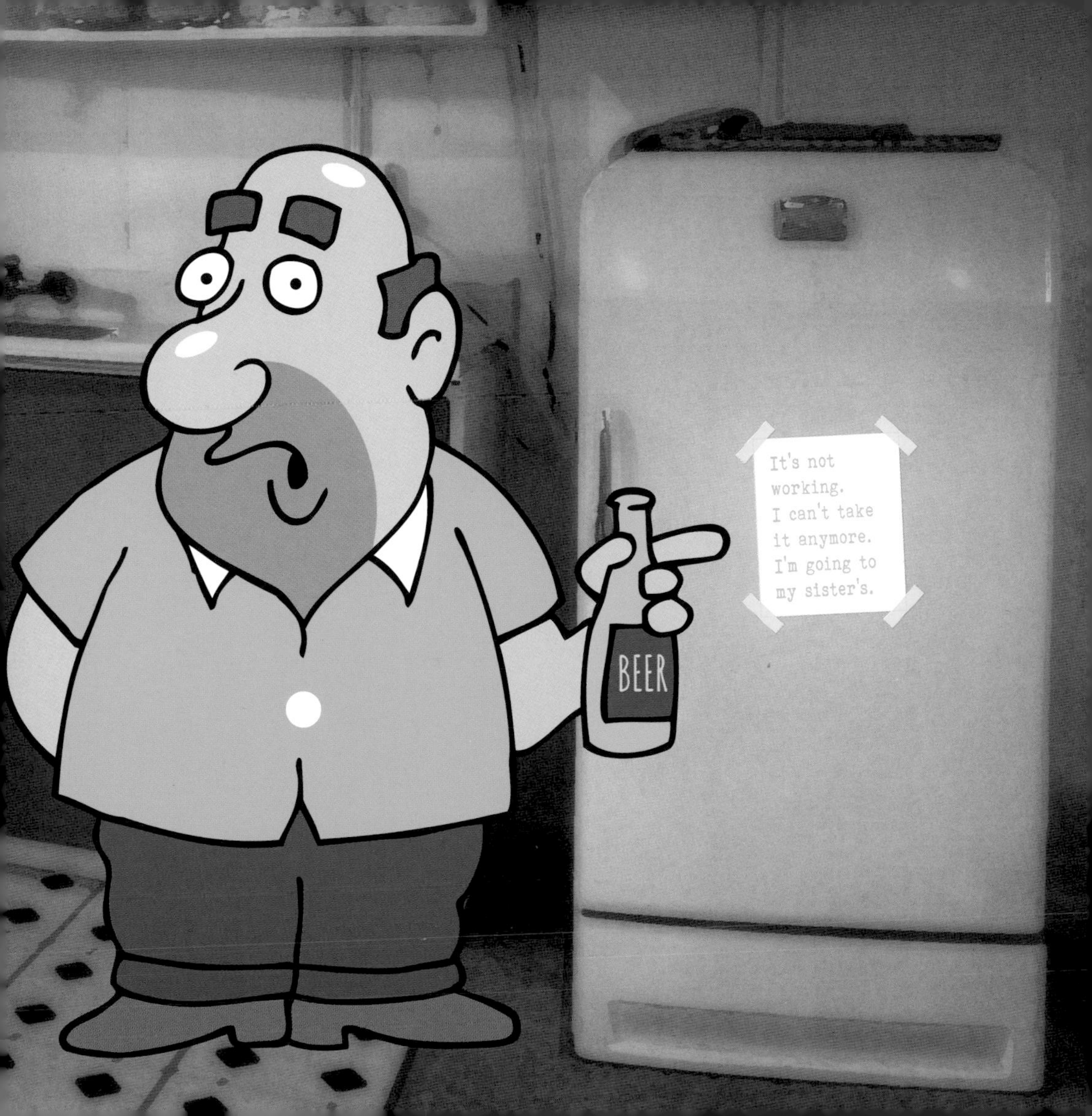
BEER
It's not
working.
I can't take
it anymore.
I'm going to
my sister's.

Men are like **FINE WINE.**
They start out as grapes,
then it's our job to
stomp on them
and keep them
in the dark
until they
mature into
something
you'd like to
have
dinner
with.

For all those men who say,
"Why buy the cow
when you can get milk for free?"
Here's an update for you...
Nowadays 80% of women are
against marriage. Why?

Because women
realize it's not
worth buying an
entire pig just to
get a little
sausage.

I am sweet, lovable, kind, shy and innocent...

...oh for heaven's sake! Stop laughing.

The cost of living is getting so high,

she is having sex with **ME** because she can't afford the cost of batteries.

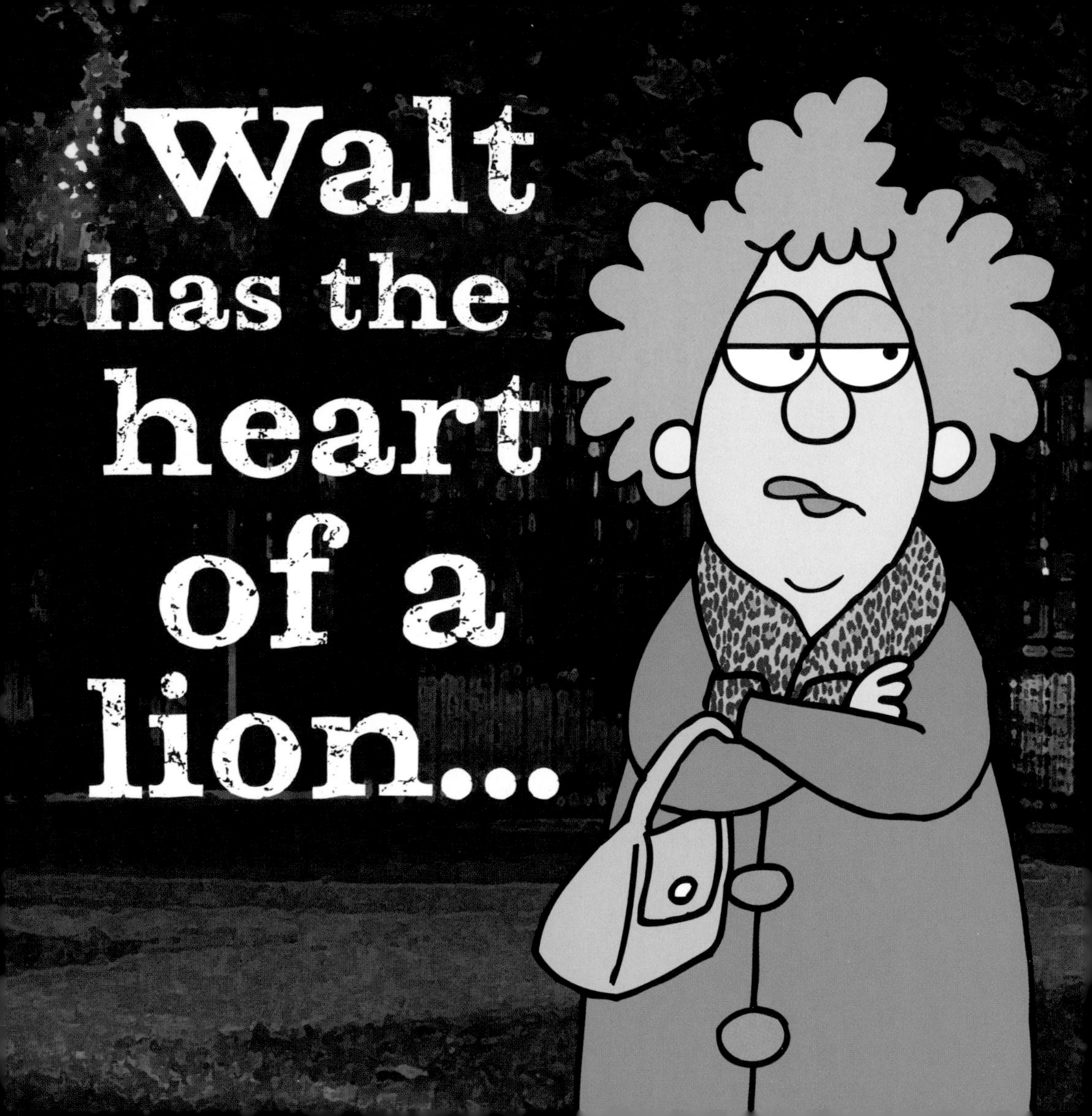
Walt has the heart of a lion...

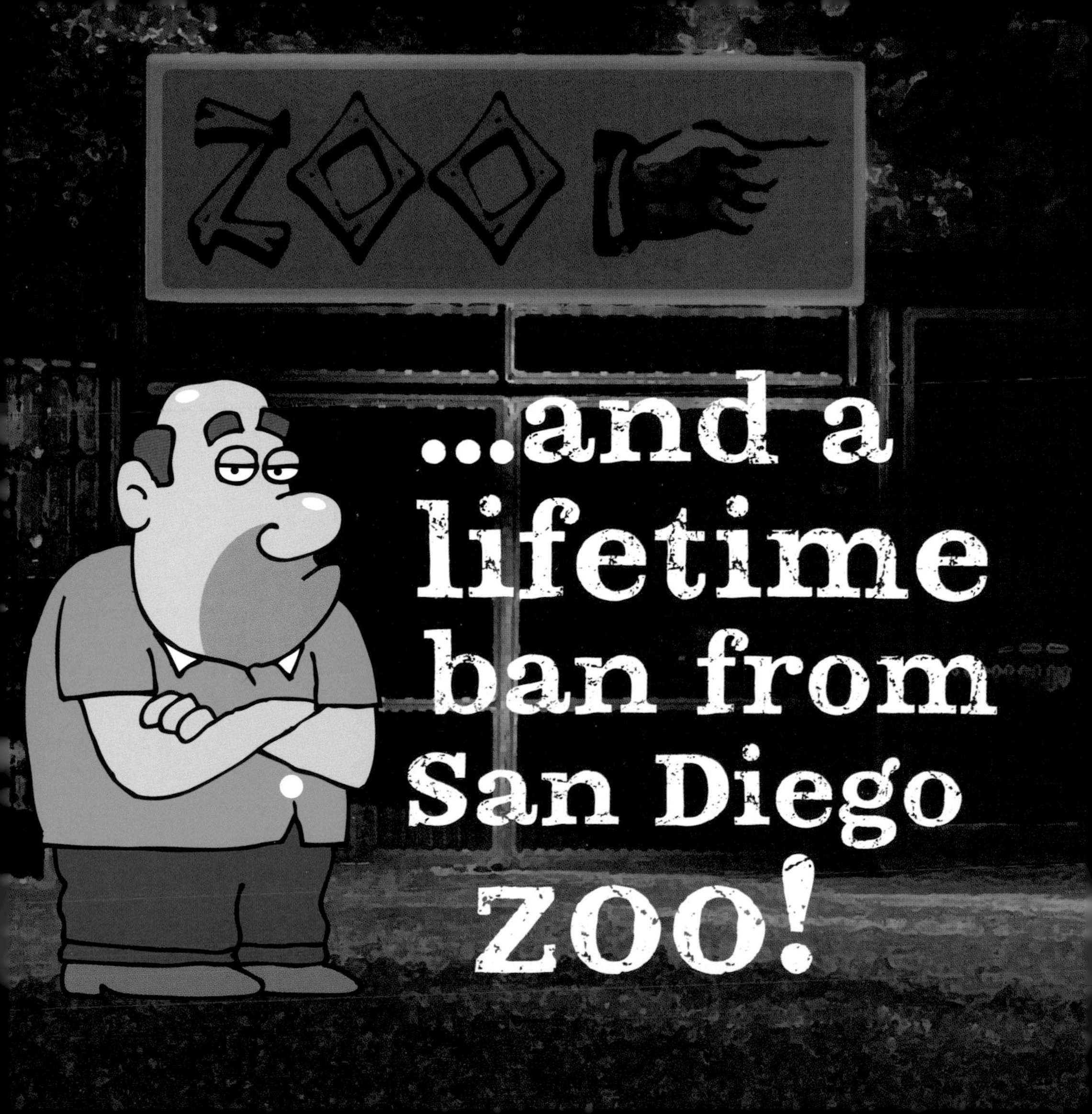
ZOO
...and a lifetime ban from San Diego ZOO!

Walt's always whining about how I'm suffocating him. I think, if I can hear him whining, I'm not pressing down hard enough on the pillow.

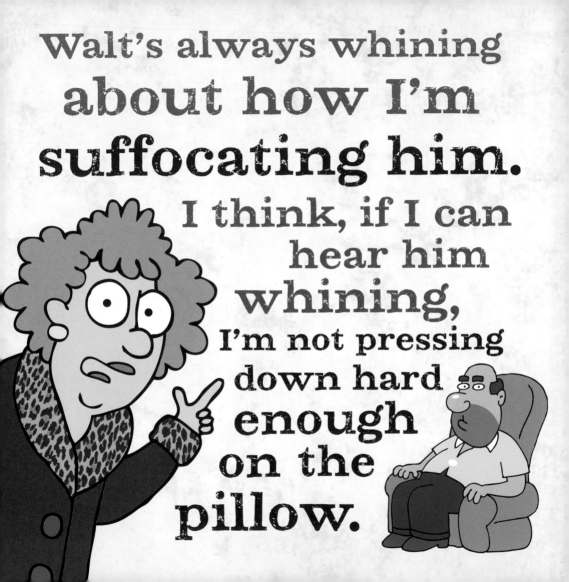

They say, "Dress for the job you want, not for the job you have."

So I've started going to work dressed as

Ryan Gosling's wife.

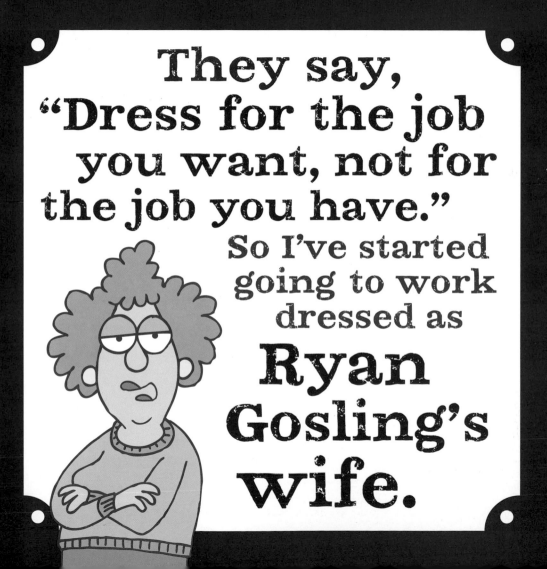

Some people come into
our lives and leave
footprints on
our hearts...
Others come along
and we want
to leave
footprints
on
their
face.

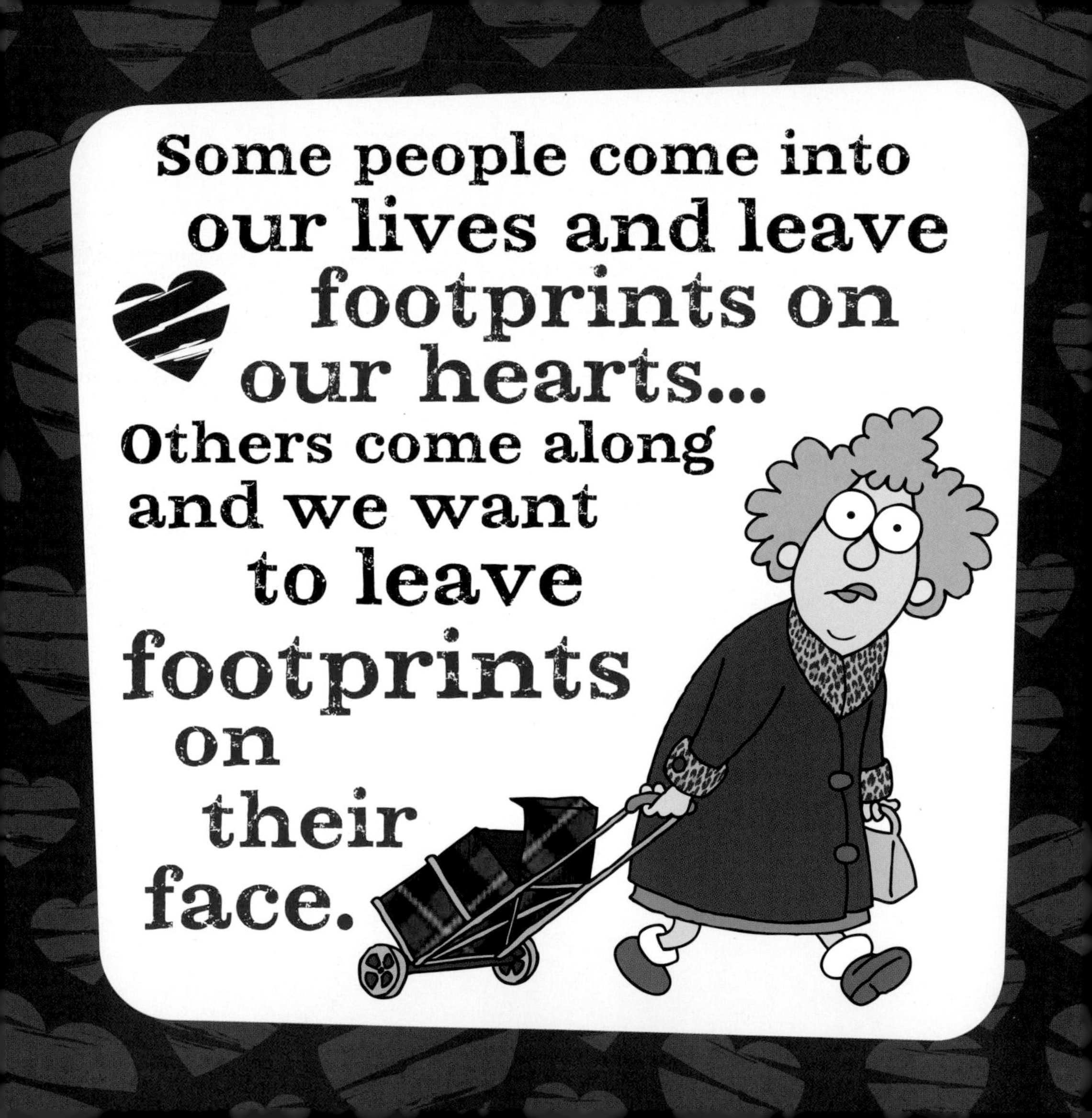

Last night I said to my wife, "I never want to become a vegetable, dependent on some machine and fluids from a bottle to keep me alive. That would be no quality of life at all. If that ever happens, just pull the plug."

So she got up, unplugged the TV and threw out my beer.

PAIN MAKES YOU STRONGER.
TEARS MAKE YOU BRAVER.
A BROKEN HEART MAKES YOU WISER.

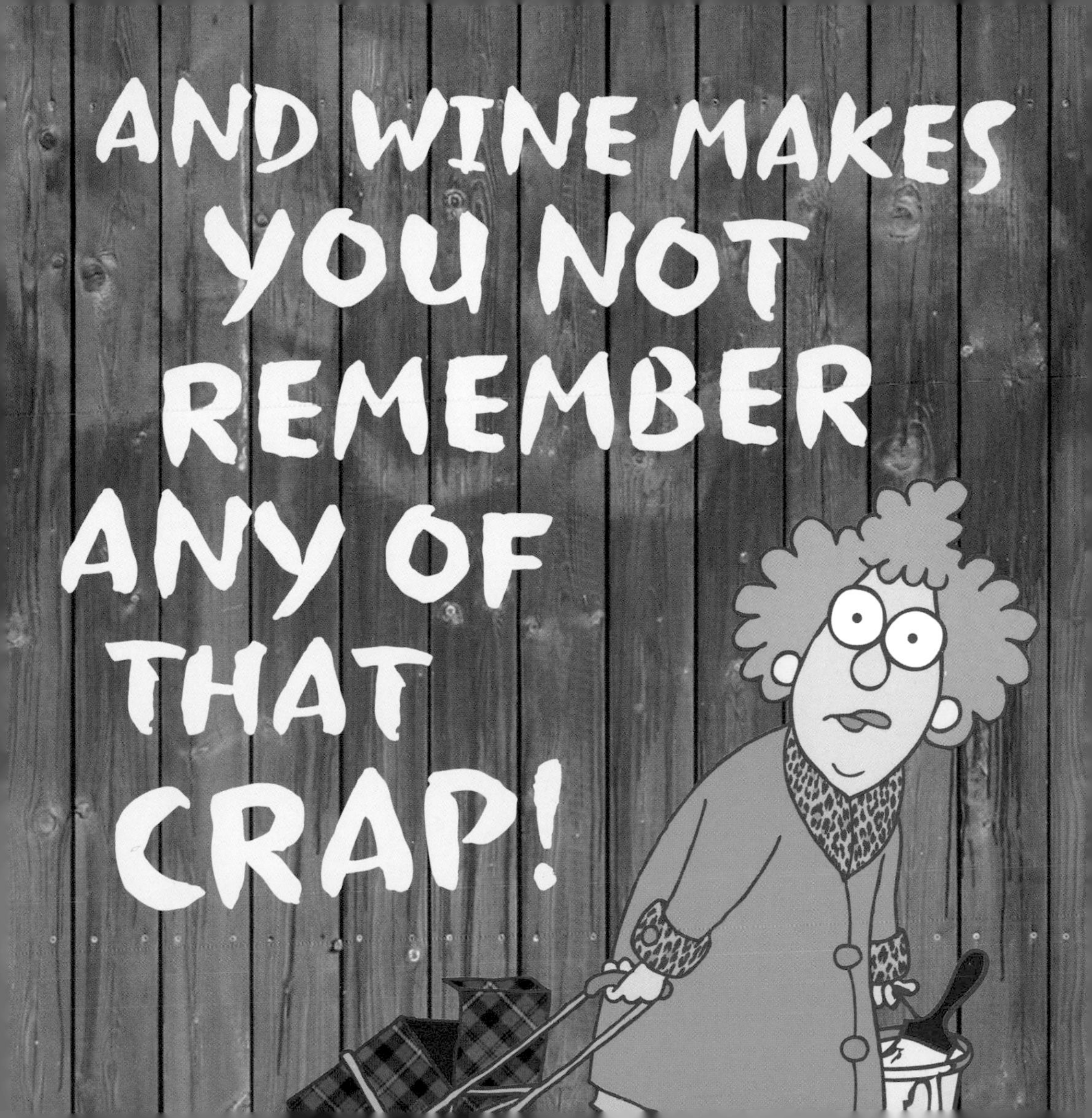
AND WINE MAKES
YOU NOT
REMEMBER
ANY OF
THAT
CRAP!

Men are like **mascara...**

They usually **run at** the first **sign of** emotion.

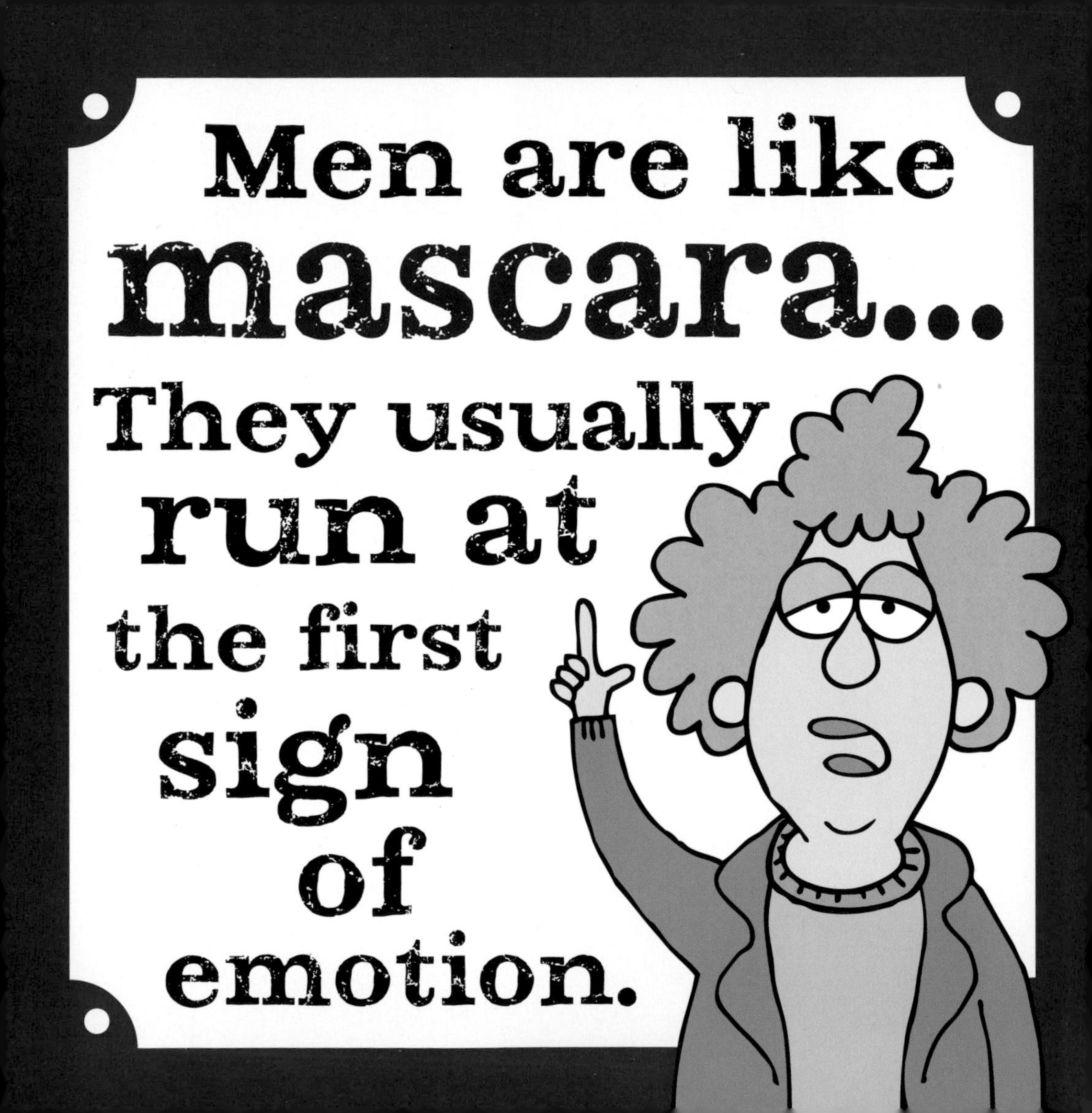

Chocolate.

It's like sex you don't have to shave your legs for.

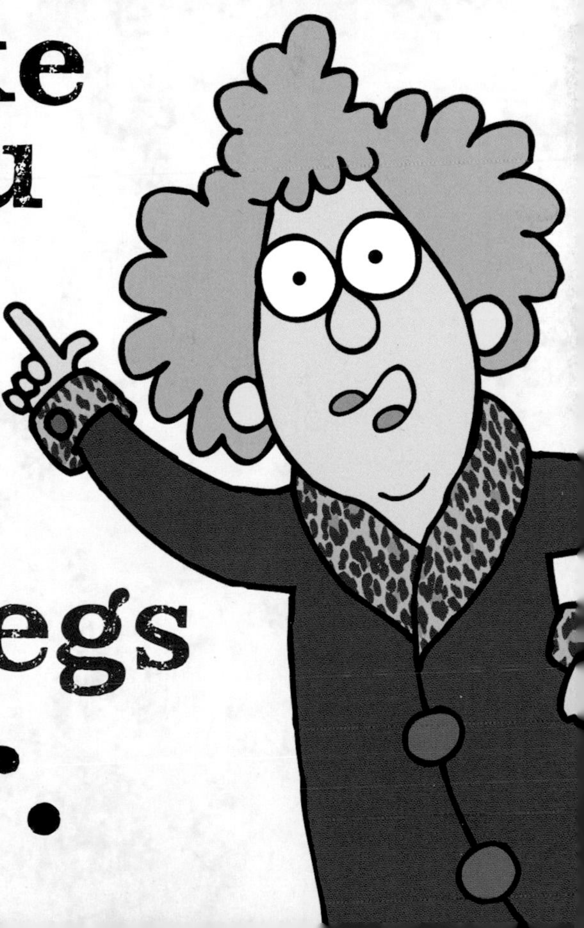

I suppose you could say Walt and I have a "Romeo and Juliet" romance.

He can't stand my parents and I wish he'd accidentally drink poison.

AUNTY ACID'S TEENAGE ADVICE NO.16

The best place to break up with your girlfriend is a

FAST FOOD RESTAURANT

There're no sharp knives or forks and you can always hide behind a fat kid.

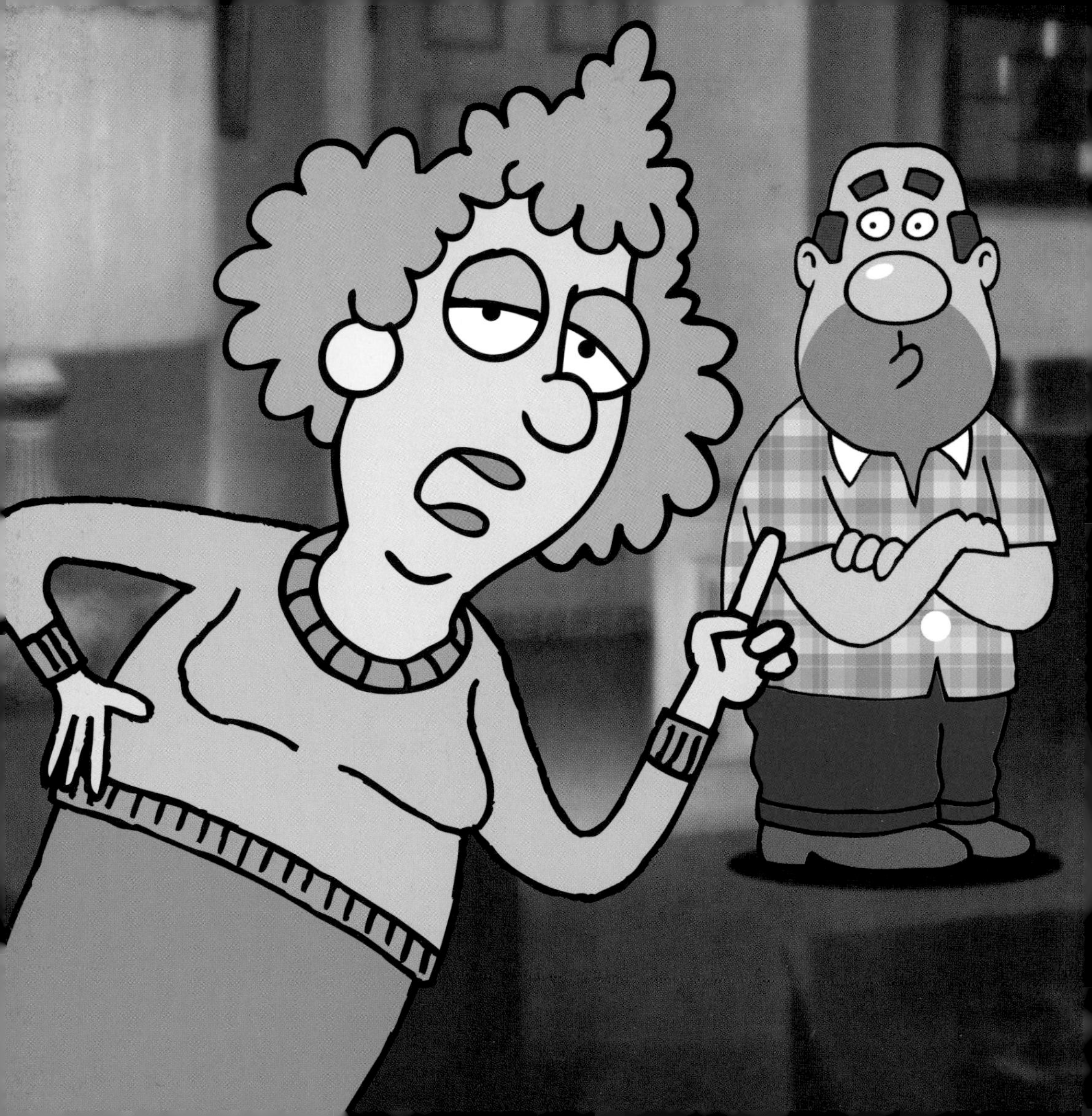

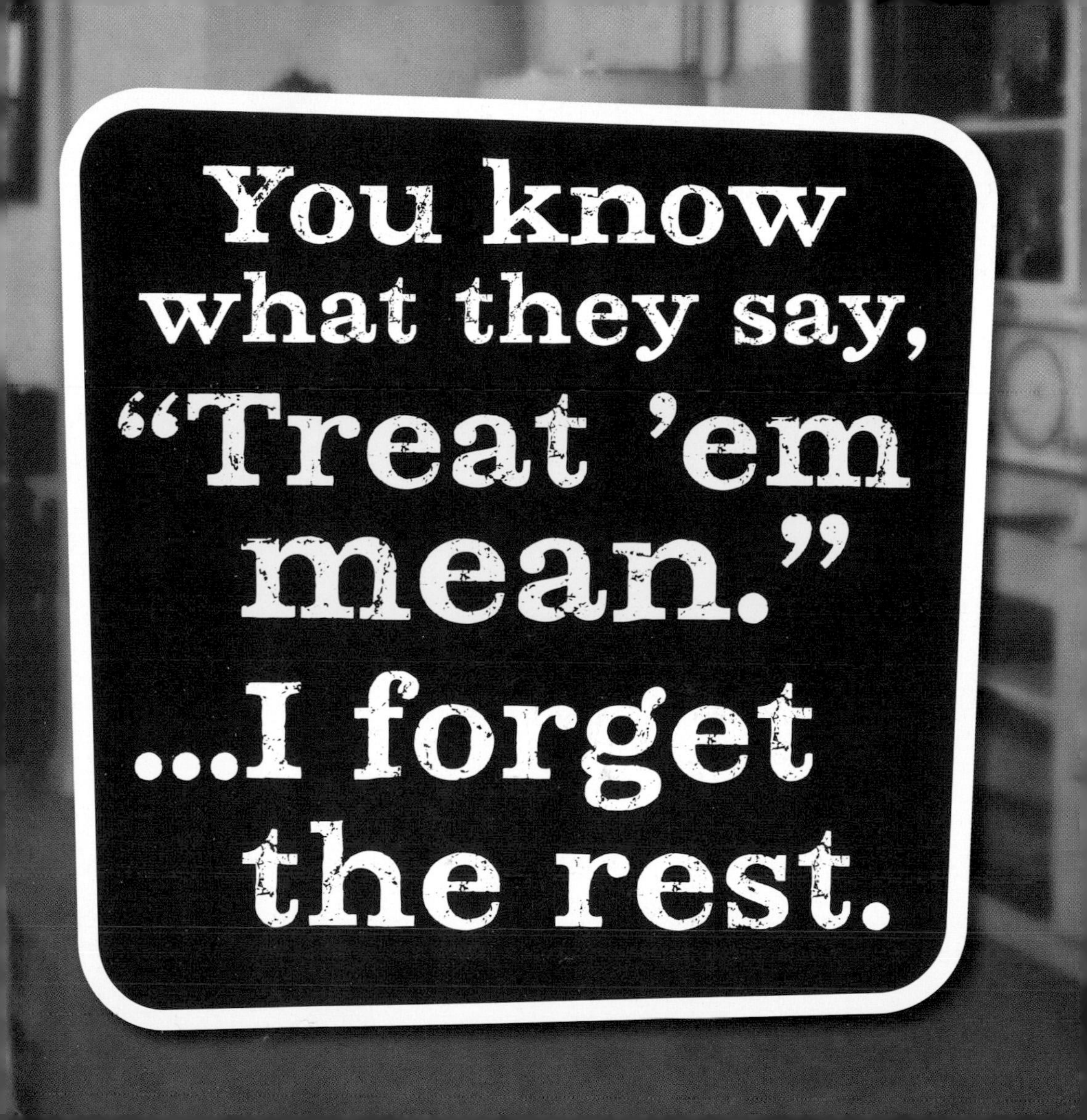
You know
what they say,
"Treat 'em
mean."
...I forget
the rest.

First Edition
17 16 15 14 13   5 4 3 2

Published by
Gibbs Smith
P.O. Box 667
Layton, Utah 84041

1.800.835.4993 orders
www.gibbs-smith.com

Illustrations by Dave Iddon @ The Backland Studio
Interiors designed by Dave Iddon
Cover designed by Melissa Dymock
Printed and bound in China

Gibbs Smith books are printed on either
recycled, 100% post-consumer waste, FSC-
certified papers or on paper produced from
sustainable PEFC-certified forest/controlled
wood source. Learn more at www.pefc.org.

ISBN 13: 978-1-4236-3497-3